MW01486885

THE COURAGEOUS
POLICE
LEADER

A Survival Guide for Combating
Cowards, Chaos & Lies

Written by Travis Yates with JC Chaix

Foreword by Stacy Ettel

Published by Stoic Publishing

2019

CONTENTS

© 2019 Travis Yates

ISBN 978-1-7331605-9-9 (Paperback)

Cataloging in Publication Data
Travis Yates
The Courageous Police Leader: A Survival Guide for Combating Cowards, Chaos, and Lies; Travis Yates; ISBN 978-1-7331605-9-9

Library of Congress Control Number 2019906303

This book contains opinions intended for law enforcement training and educational purposes.

Edited by JC Chaix

Published by STOIC Publishing

www.stopcowards.com

First Edition

10 9 8 7 6 5 4 3 2 1

FOREWORD

I really didn't think about the damage that cowardly police leaders can do until March 2, 2010. I was a 39-year-old police commander with 17 years on the job. My dreams had come true, my retirement was just around the corner, and my future was on the rise. For me, life was as good as it gets.

But all that changed in ways I couldn't imagine. As the commander on duty, I responded to a disturbance involving a subject struggling with mental health issues. Negotiations were underway, but I put together a team of officers to prepare for the worst, according to protocol and procedures we used to successfully resolve similar incidents in the past.

Unfortunately, the subject was uncooperative and unwilling to negotiate. We evacuated the building. And when our team went in, we soon encountered a defiant, aggressively violent subject. We used every tactic available from verbal commands, to bean bags, and a Taser, and other less-lethal options. But the subject refused to cooperate and still refused to drop the knife. And then it happened: when the subject threatened officers with the knife, an officer used deadly force to stop the threat.

It was the ending nobody wanted. But as the commander, I was certain that we did everything we could to prevent the use of deadly force. A school administrator who witnessed the ordeal praised our team for our diligence, our compassion, and our professionalism. The shooting was not fatal.

I went home that night to a loving family and supportive wife. I assured them that everything was going to be alright, thinking that I could rely on my superiors and leaders for support. However, I would soon discover just how rare courageous leadership had become.

The protests began immediately. And even before the formal investigations started, the news media was already blaming "five racist cops" for unnecessarily shooting a black foreign-exchange student. Our efforts, our compassion, and the facts didn't seem to matter. We had no idea about the subject's race, and we had absolutely no idea about the subject's visa status. And weeks later, when the subject pled guilty to assaulting police officers that didn't seem to matter either. The protests continued.

Months went by and I couldn't help feeling ostracized. The shooting was cleared by the top state law enforcement agency, the United States Department of Justice, and the Department of Education. And that's when I became fully aware of the damage that cowardly leadership can do. The higher-ups wanted to terminate the officer who fired the shot. They asked me to support this decision. When I refused, my own contract was terminated.

My career was gone.

The months and years that followed would prove to be the darkest times for my family. I applied for over 100 jobs. And even though I was the top pick for more than a few, I was told that it would be too risky to hire me due to everything the media said about me.

I lost my pension.

I lost my house.

At one point, my wife even sold her wedding ring so we could afford food for a few more weeks.

However, despite all the damage that cowardly leaders can cause, I never gave up hope that someone would boldly look beyond the lies. I finally applied for a deputy position, and sure enough, a truly courageous leader came through. The sheriff put aside the nonsense, and understood full well that I still had plenty of years ahead of me to serve others to the benefit of his community. I was hired as a sheriff's deputy and began to put the shattered pieces of my life back together.

About five years after that fateful night, I sat across from Travis Yates and told him my story. Travis was awestruck by what I had suffered due to cowardly leadership. And even though we just met, telling my story became a personal mission for him. This book does just that and so much more.

At the very least, I hope this book will serve as a warning to everyone who wears a badge. If I had read what's written in these pages before March 2, 2010, I would have foreseen the chaos. I would have understood the lies. I would have done more to put a stop to cowardly leadership.

Regrettably, there are too many stories like mine and there will likely be more in the future. But I find comfort in knowing that this book may help others combat the cowards, the chaos, and the lies—and may inspire courageous leaders to stay in the fight.

—Stacy Ettel

INTRODUCTION

The law enforcement profession is in crisis—and the blame lies with cowardly police leaders, political "reformers," social justice "warriors," and all the chaos they create. The job is tough enough. Yet cowardly police leaders have made things worse—far worse. From blindly following political agendas, to making absurd policy revisions, to appeasing the shouting few without credibility or expertise to make demands, it's a wonder that anyone shows up for duty anymore. Yet when they do, far too many law enforcement professionals waste valuable time and energy dealing with infighting, instead of crime-fighting.

This must stop.

But it's going to take a lot more Courageous Police Leaders to put a stop to all the nonsense. They're the ones who stay focused on crime despite all the nonsense and chaos. They're the ones who stay focused on policing instead of politics. And above all, they're the ones who sacrifice to serve others, even with their own lives.

Absolutely, it's going to take a lot of courage to send the cowards running. And it's going to take a lot of courage and perseverance to get America refocused on fighting crime and making real progress toward a better future. Fortunately, law enforcement has always summoned the courage to overcome the worst kinds of evil and all kinds of adversity. Ever since the city of Boston established the first professional police department back in 1838, the law enforcement profession has been making progress.

Granted, there have been plenty of misdeeds, plenty of embarrassing instances of misconduct, and plenty of rough patches. But overall, the law enforcement profession has evolved for the better in the past two centuries.

Personally speaking, the profession has made tremendous progress since my grandfather-in-law became a police officer back in 1940. It's come a long way since my father started his law enforcement career in 1972. And it's improved considerably since I joined the ranks in 1993. Whether it's better training, safer equipment, or the evolution of case law to better protect the rights of citizens, law enforcement has been heading in the right direction. In the last decade, however, the profession has become stuck in a downward spiral.

CRISIS MODE

Some say law enforcement has been in crisis mode since the Rodney King incident in 1991. Others point to the riots in Ferguson, Missouri in 2014. Both of these unfortunate incidents were pivotal moments. Although, perhaps the most profound undoing of the law enforcement profession occurred in 2009 with the uttering of a single sentence.

First, let's briefly cover the backstory. On July 16, 2009, Harvard professor Henry Louis Gates Jr. returned to his residence in Cambridge, Massachusetts after taking a trip to China. While Gates was away, his front door got stuck and he couldn't get in. He asked his driver for help, and as they were struggling with the door, someone called the Cambridge Police Department to report a possible burglary in progress.

In response—that is, because someone called 911 to report a possible crime—Cambridge Police Sergeant James Crowley was dispatched to the residence. Sergeant Crowley, in telling his side of the story, stated that "Professor Gates, a prolific scholar of African-American history, had been oddly belligerent from the start of their encounter."[1] Sergeant Crowley recalled that when he asked Professor Gates to come outside and talk, Gates said, "Yeah, I'll speak with your mama outside." And after repeatedly warning Gates to stop yelling and causing a disturbance outside the residence, Sergeant Crowley arrested Gates for disorderly conduct.

Both Professor Gates and Sergeant Crowley probably had no idea this encounter would set off a nationwide debate. And they probably had no idea that President Barack Obama would offer his opinion about the incident during a national news conference:

> "I don't know, not having been there and not seeing all the facts, what role race played, but I think it's fair to say, number one, any of us would be pretty angry; number two, that the Cambridge police acted stupidly in arresting somebody when there was already proof that they were in their own home; and, number three... that there's a long history in this country of African-Americans and Latinos being stopped by law enforcement disproportionately." [2]

Did you notice what happened?

---

[1] Abby Goodnough, "Sergeant Who Arrested Professor Defends Actions," *The New York Times,* July 24, 2009.

[2] Matt Spetalnick, "Obama: Police Acted 'Stupidly' Arresting Black Scholar," *Reuters,* July 22, 2009.

With just one sentence, albeit a long-winded one, the president of the United States turned a misdemeanor arrest into a matter of racial politics and national concern. President Obama admitted to "not seeing all the facts." Nonetheless, the president didn't question *if* race played a role, he questioned *"what role* race played." It may seem subtle, but his choice of words is remarkably significant.

It didn't take long for President Obama 's assumptions to become an indictment of law enforcement professionals across the nation. And while the president's questioning of racial discrimination may seem subtle, his insult about how the police "acted stupidly" is nothing but obvious. Yet even more obvious is the president's lack of understanding about law enforcement, which is underscored by his comment about "being stopped."

Obviously, Sergeant Crowley didn't "stop" anybody—he responded to a 911 call. And every law enforcement professional in America knows the difference between a "stop" and a "call." But judging by the president's remarks and public reaction, the difference doesn't seem to matter—but the difference is extremely important.

For the record, a "stop," like stopping a car for a traffic violation, is a *pro-active* law enforcement activity, and officers have some discretion in being pro-active. However, responding to a "call," like Sergeant Crowley was dispatched to the Gates residence, is *reactive*—and officers inherit the circumstances. Whenever officers respond to a 911 call, they have nothing to do with who is involved, what's going on, or who called or why.

Just to be clear, Sergeant Crowley had nothing to do with the circumstances or the reason for the 911 call. He had nothing to do with the demographic profile of anyone involved. He had nothing to do with the condition of the door, the color of the house, or any other circumstance—as a law enforcement officer, Sergeant Crowley was dispatched to the location to do his job.

While President Obama's lack of understanding about a "stop" and a "call" seems baffling, his final remark seems even more confused—and deeply concerning. The president's claim that "there's a long history in this country of African-Americans and Latinos being stopped by law enforcement disproportionately" seems dubious. Such a remark contradicts the facts about traffic stops, including those reported by the United States Bureau of Justice Statistics, for example: "In 2008, white, black, and Hispanic drivers were stopped by police at similar rates."[3]

However, President Obama's claim about "African-Americans and Latinos being stopped by law enforcement disproportionately" draws something quite significant into question—"disproportionately" to what? Did President Obama mean "disproportionately" as in the absurd notion there should be parity between demography and crime?

---

[3] Christine Eith and Matthew R. Durose, *Contacts Between Police And The Public, 2008,* United States Department of Justice, Bureau of Justice Statistics, October 5, 2011, NCJ 234599.

Does anyone actually believe that if a demographic group makes up 10 percent of a community, they could only commit 10 percent of the crimes? What happens if this group is responsible for more than 10 percent—should law enforcement just let them go? Should 911 dispatchers simply hang up once the "suspect quota" based on demographic parity is reached? And does a law enforcement agency automatically become racist if a demographic group represents 10 percent of the community, yet people in this group are suspects in 10.01 percent, or 11 percent or 50 percent of the crimes?

Putting absurdity aside, the president's claim about the "long history" is about the only thing that's accurate—although probably not for the purpose he intended. Indeed, many have mistakenly believed for quite a long time that "affirmative action" somehow applies to crime. And even if it did, it should apply to the criminals who commit crimes—not to the officers who respond to them.

Whatever the president meant, he quickly seemed to realize that he misspoke. Two days later, he explained to reporters at the White House:

> "...because this has been ratcheting up, and I obviously helped contribute ratcheting it up, I want to make clear that in my choice of words I think I unfortunately gave an impression that I was maligning the Cambridge Police Department or Sergeant Crowley specifically—and I could have calibrated those words differently. And I told this to Sergeant Crowley."[4]

---

[4] Michael Fletcher and Michael Shear, "Obama Voices Regret to Policeman," *The Washington Post,* July 25, 2009.

"Calibration" isn't the only thing wrong in accusing the law enforcement profession throughout America of upholding "a long history" of racial discrimination. However, the president's "sort-of apology" sure seems like a good example of an over-complicated way to admit to making unfounded accusations. And it sure does seem like a cowardly way to accept responsibility for inflaming racial tensions throughout the nation—by ignoring facts and pointing the finger at the law enforcement profession.

Unfortunately, the president didn't stop there. Instead, he continued with even more confusing and hypocritical remarks:

> "And even when you've got a police officer who has a fine track record on racial sensitivity, interactions between police officers and the African-American community can sometimes be fraught with misunderstanding."

Just in case this needs to be said, this wasn't an incident that involved the "African-American community"—it involved one frustrated citizen and one arresting officer. And if there was any "misunderstanding" in this case, it was the police who were misunderstood—as President Obama's "apology" clearly indicates. Yet this shouldn't seem surprising considering the first words the president uttered about this case: "I don't know..."

So just to be clear, if this incident was "fraught with misunderstanding," it was brought on by the president's assumptions, his ridiculing law enforcement in front of the national media, and his misplaced notion of crime and affirmative action.

In trying to backpedal, President Obama concluded:

> "My hope is that as a consequence of this event, this ends up being
> what's called a teachable moment, where all of us, instead of
> pumping up the volume, spend a little more time listening to each
> other and try to focus on how we can generally improve relations
> between police officers and minority communities, and that instead
> of flinging accusations, we can all be a little more reflective, in terms
> of what we can do to contribute to more unity."

Indeed, this was a "teachable moment." For one thing, it can teach us a
valuable lesson about how news and social media can divide us. And it can
also teach every politician, every cowardly leader, and every "reformer" a
lesson about the chaos they may cause whenever they ignore facts, make
assumptions, and hurl unfounded accusations at law enforcement.

A BLUEPRINT FOR CRITICIZING THE POLICE

Of course, like every other American, the president is entitled to an opinion.
And if such opinion shames the law enforcement profession, then so be it.
However, the problem isn't that President Obama had an opinion. The
problem is that the president of the United States clearly demonstrated that
facts aren't necessary to criticize law enforcement officers, or to insult them,
or to suggest that they're racist. If this was a "teachable" moment, these seem
to be the take-aways. And in hindsight, it's difficult to ignore how President
Obama's rhetoric seems to have become a "blueprint" or a textbook for
criticizing law enforcement and undermining law enforcement efforts.

Quickly sketched out, it looks something like this:

1. *Ignore the facts*: it's OK if you "don't know, not having been there and not seeing all the facts"—facts aren't necessary;

2. *Be angry with law enforcement*: "any of us would be pretty angry"— especially since being angry with law enforcement now seems to be sanctioned by the president;

3. *Insist that what you believe happened is true*: never mind any other explanations, or facts or evidence—*your opinion* is the only thing that matters;

4. *Use vague historical or statistical claims for "legitimacy"*: claiming that the police "acted stupidly in arresting somebody" sounds better when it has something to do with "a long history in this country..."—even if actual facts and stats prove otherwise.

Unfortunately for America, ever since the Cambridge incident, and the media frenzy that followed, far too many unfounded criticisms of law enforcement seem to bear an uncanny resemblance to this "blueprint."[5]

SPINNING OUT OF CONTROL...

If the downward spiral began in Cambridge in 2009, it seems things began spinning completely out of control in Ferguson, Missouri in 2014, when robbery suspect Michael Brown attacked Officer Darren Wilson—and lies, myths, and chaos ensued. Subsequently, law enforcement has been subjected

---

[5] For example, the backlash in Ferguson, Missouri (August 2014); Baltimore (April 2015); St. Paul (August 2016); Chicago (July 2018); and many other regrettable incidents in between.

to relentless waves of "reform" ever since. For example, the Obama administration investigated 25 police departments throughout the nation.[6] These federal investigations involved different circumstances and different law enforcement agencies—yet many of the "reforms" strangely have a lot in common. Some of the common "reforms" included:

> *Revising police policies*—shifting away from the standards set by case law and Supreme Court decisions to more stringent and restrictive protocols, and pseudo legislation;
>
> *Revamping police training programs*—as if "de-escalation" and avoiding the use of force are always necessary, even when officers are confronted by violent criminals who refuse to comply;
>
> *Reorganizing police command and oversight committees*—as though civilians are experts and keenly understand the problems with law enforcement and the criminal justice system, and know precisely how to solve them without making things worse;
>
> *Rescinding funds and budgets for police equipment*—to prevent law enforcement from appearing too "militaristic," despite the growing need to control increasingly violent disturbances, riots, and attacks on law enforcement officers;
>
> *Requiring body cameras*—to show first-hand what is "wrong" with law enforcement, and prosecute and punish law enforcement officers.

---

[6] Candice Norwood, "Why California Is a Case Study for Monitoring Police Misconduct," *The Atlantic*, May 24, 2017.

Progress is one thing. However, much like President Obama's unfounded criticism and implied racial bias, many of the "reforms" that followed in the aftermath of Ferguson were not based on facts and evidence. Instead, they were based predominantly on misbeliefs, myths, and flat-out lies. Yes, despite all the attention in the news and on social media, the "Hands Up, Don't Shoot" mantra was based on a lie—and all of the "necessary reforms" that were demanded were based on a lie as well.

Contrary to the myth-making of the social justice "warriors" who protested and rioted in Ferguson, including the protestors who were paid to be there,[7] the U.S. Department of Justice (DOJ) cleared Officer Wilson of any civil rights violations. Instead of relying on assumptions and accusations, the DOJ conducted an exhaustive investigation based on facts and evidence.[8] The St. Louis County grand jury, conducted its own separate investigation, and also found no cause to indict Officer Wilson after its own extensive review of the circumstances, facts and evidence. And after conducting yet another independent investigation of the incident, the Federal Bureau of Investigation (FBI) also cleared Officer Wilson after analyzing the facts and evidence as well.

---

[7] Kelly Riddel, "George Soros Funds Ferguson Protests, Hopes to Spur Civil Action," *The Washington Times*, January 14, 2015.

[8] United States Department of Justice. *Department of Justice Report Regarding the Criminal Investigation into the Shooting Death of Michael Brown by Ferguson, Missouri Police Officer Darren Wilson*, (Washington D.C.: Department of Justice, 2015).

So let's be absolutely clear. While social justice "warriors," news reporters, and politicians were supporting the myth behind the "Hands Up, Don't Shoot" mantra, the DOJ, the St. Louis County grand jury, and the FBI all independently concluded that Michael Brown was not surrendering with his "hands up" when he attacked Officer Wilson. And in stark contrast to the catchy protest slogan, the FBI examined the facts and evidence and determined that the first shot was fired at close range while Brown was attacking Officer Wilson.

Indeed, facts and evidence can be quite useful. And in this case, the evidence and facts examined by the FBI clearly prove how the "Hands Up, Don't Shoot" movement was based on a lie. Yet unfortunately for America, there have been few attempts to set the record straight about this falsehood and how a robbery suspect attacked a police officer in Ferguson, Missouri. Although some courageous leaders, activists, and journalists have tried to set the record straight without much success. For example, in 2015, Jonathan Capehart of The Washington Post, made one of the earliest attempts to point out that "Hands Up, Don't Shoot" was built on a lie.[9] Capehart demonstrated exemplary courage when he insisted that:

> "we must never allow ourselves to march under the banner of a false narrative on behalf of someone who would otherwise offend our sense of right and wrong."

---

[9] Jonatahan Capehart, "Hands Up, Don't Shoot"" Was Built on a Lie," *The Washington Post*, March 16, 2015.

Despite his remarkable insight, and courage to argue against popular opinion, Capehart and others were still trying to explain the lies—and still trying to get people to just consider the evidence in the DOJ report even two years later.[10] It's pretty astounding, especially considering that facts and evidence are the bedrock of the criminal justice system, along with science, medicine, and other critical fields that we depend upon for life, liberty, and well-being.

Nonetheless, for those who are trying to fabricate myths and brainwash America, facts and evidence are far too inconvenient and bothersome. Or maybe all the social justice "warriors" are just too busy or politically invested to reconsider the facts and evidence concerning their "unarmed black man shot by white cop" narrative. Likewise, it seems cowardly police leaders have been way too busy implementing all the "necessary reforms" to think critically and carefully as well. However, much like President Obama's "teachable moment," if the events in Ferguson can teach us anything, it's this: cowardly police leaders are part of the problem, if not the cause.

In hindsight, it's clear that the aftermath of Ferguson had little to do with the facts about an officer defending himself against a violent attack, but had everything to do with cowards, chaos, and lies. This was laid bare when the DOJ report exonerated Wilson—but condemned the leadership of the Ferguson city government, the municipal court system, and the police department.

---

[10] Jonathan Capehart, "Standing by My Opinion That 'Hands Up, Don't Shoot' Was Built on a Lie," *The Washington Post,* March 16, 2017.

In other words, the problem wasn't that a police officer defended himself. The bigger problem was a mixture of cowardly police leadership and misguided politics. And once again, politicians and the national news media could have set the record straight. But instead, they quietly tip-toed away from personally attacking Officer Wilson, to attacking the "underlying problems" as though the blame had never been misplaced.[11] Officer Wilson's career was swept up in a whirlwind of lies, politics, social "justice" and cowardly leadership.

So, let's be courageous for a moment and set the record straight. Officer Darren Wilson was a victim of a violent attack—and a victim of cowardly leadership, despite the courageous efforts of those who tried to help. Wilson's unfortunate experience should underscore the problems with cowardly police leadership in America. Every time law enforcement professionals like Wilson must resign for presumed wrongdoing—despite facts and evidence to the contrary—cowardly police leaders are forsaking the truth and propping up false narratives and lies. Every time officers are terminated as scapegoats to "keep up appearances," cowardly police leaders are damaging the reputation of every law enforcement professional throughout the nation. And every time these things happen, it's more likely that any one of us will be the next victim of cowardly police leadership— because we are not standing up together to combat the cowards, the chaos, and the lies.

---

[11] For example, see Jeremey Kohler, "Justice Report Calls Ferguson Municipal Court an Abusive Fundraising Tool, *St. Louis Post-Dispatch,* March 4, 2015.

It's time to send cowardly police leaders running to another line of work, or early retirement—anywhere else so long as the cowards know that the law enforcement profession is no longer a comfortable place to cower and hide. There's absolutely no reason why courageous law enforcement professionals should tolerate them any longer. Besides, they were never welcome in the profession in the first place. The time for Courageous Police Leaders to reclaim the law enforcement profession—and get back to fighting crime and truly making a difference is long overdue.

Admittedly, if we had more Courageous Police Leaders, this book wouldn't be necessary. But unfortunately, it is necessary since hardly a week goes by without "outrage" and accusations being aimed at law enforcement professionals across the nation—along with all the rocks and bottles, and demands for "justice," and "reform" in some form or another.

And while this is also painful to admit, as law enforcement professionals, we have collectively failed—we've let cowardly leaders endanger the lives and careers of courageous professionals for far too long. It seems we've become too apathetic, and too concerned about saving our own necks, instead of upholding our duty and our mission to serve with honor, dignity, and integrity. Yet there is no honor, no dignity, and no integrity in allowing cowardly police leaders to get away with the problems they create. And in this regard, we've failed to become a collective force of courageous police leaders in combating the (self-proclaimed) enemies of law enforcement.

Bear in mind, courageous police leadership isn't about rank—it's everyone's responsibility. A Courageous Police Leader can be a cop, a deputy, a chief, a corporal, a sheriff—anyone who has had enough of the unfounded accusations, unsafe compromises, and cowardly leadership.

We are absolutely a formidable, collective force because any one of us is capable of being a Courageous Police Leader. And much like the ancient wisdom of Sun Tzu's *Art of War*, being a Courageous Police Leader takes a fearless commitment to:

1. knowing your enemies;
2. knowing yourself; and
3. being courageous no matter what the challenges may be.

Hopefully, this book will help you focus on these aspects—and hopefully, it will help inspire your courage. But beware, if you turn the page there is no return. So proceed with caution as you read on and take your place among other courageous men and women in law enforcement—and become a more formidable enemy of all the cowards, the chaos and the lies.

Major Travis Yates, MS
ILEETA Police Trainer of the Year
CEO, Courageous Leadership Institute
Editor-In-Chief, Law Officer Magazine

PART I

KNOW
YOUR
ENEMY

THE NO.1 ENEMY OF LAW ENFORCEMENT

"If you know the enemy and know yourself,
you need not fear the outcome of a hundred battles." —*Sun Tzu*

The ancient wisdom of Chinese military strategist Sun Tzu has inspired courageous leaders for thousands of years. So it would be wise to follow such advice, and start by getting to know the number one enemy of law enforcement: the cowardly police leader.

That's right, many of our so-called leaders are in fact our worst enemies. And there are plenty of reasons why cowardly leaders are the archenemy of law enforcement. For starters, instead of guarding the proverbial castle, cowardly leaders let social justice "warriors" stroll through the front gate to announce their demands. And instead of motivating and inspiring others, cowardly leaders kill morale at every turn. Making matters even worse, cowardly police leaders aren't just the enemy, they're the enemy within. They occupy every rank and cower in every kind of law enforcement agency.

Perhaps things wouldn't be so bad if cowardly leaders only caused problems among the rank and file. Unfortunately, however, cowards create problems that extend far beyond their own agencies, and sometimes they cause problems that can ripple throughout the criminal justice system and American society. Indeed, it's not just law enforcement that suffers the consequences of cowardly leadership—victims are suffering more and more, while criminals are being punished less and less.

All of that is bad enough. But perhaps the worst thing about cowardly leaders is that we tolerate them—and we've tolerated them for way too long. It doesn't help to dwell on the past; however, it is worth noting that many of the problems cowards create could have been prevented—if only we challenged them more. So, moving forward—as a courageous, collective force—if we insist upon better leadership, the cowards will hardly stand a chance. That's because, the more we get to know and better understand our enemies, the more we can realize their weaknesses. And quite fortunately, our biggest enemy is also our weakest enemy. Even the term "cowardly leader" says a lot about their character, or the lack of it: if you're a coward, you're not a leader (aside from leading others to cower and hide from reality). But there's more to it than that. Knowing our number one enemy involves more than recognizing *who* the cowards are. It involves knowing *what* kinds of problems they cause, *how* they cause them, and *how they act— and fail to act.*

Toward better understanding these aspects, the team at the Courageous Leadership Institute has spent years analyzing cowardly leaders, and how they've failed the law enforcement profession. As part of our research, we ask law enforcement professionals who attend our Courageous Police Leadership seminars to identify and describe cowardly leaders. Despite all the different participants, from all over America, and all the different ranks and agencies, the responses have been strikingly similar. In fact, we've been able to put together a "Top 10" list of the most common, and most damaging characteristics of cowardly police leaders—the enemies within. And in following the wisdom of Sun Tzu, we would be wise to look at each of these characteristics in more detail...

TOP 10 CHARACTERISTICS OF COWARDLY POLICE LEADERS

Cowardly police leaders...

1. blame others.

2. are lazy.

3. serve themselves.

4. refuse to learn from failure.

5. do not follow a moral compass.

6. discipline inconsistently.

7. avoid necessary conflict.

8. take credit they don't deserve.

9. micro-manage.

10. are hypocrites.

1. COWARDLY LEADERS BLAME OTHERS

"Ninety-nine percent of all failures come from people who have
a habit of making excuses." —*George Washington Carver*

As many of us know all too well, cowardly leaders often blame others.
Whether it's to make themselves look good, or make others look bad,
cowards are typically the first to point the finger and blame someone else
whenever things go wrong. At the same time, they'll often do whatever it
takes to sidestep any blame, and manipulate the chain of command as
though they could never do anything wrong.

Not only do cowardly police leaders get away with blaming others, they're
often rewarded for doing so. That's because instead of taking responsibility,
cowards often serve up a scapegoat. And with all the demands for
"accountability," passing the blame and offering up a scapegoat has become
a wonderful way to pacify the latest public "outrage" swirling around on
social media at any given moment. Scapegoating also lets cowardly police
leaders seem "responsible," as though they were actually leading, and taking
action—even though doling out undeserved discipline is something that
competent, courageous leaders typically avoid.

Another thing about scapegoating that cowards seem to love is how it makes
them appear virtuous, as though they share the same values as those
demanding action or accountability. This can help explain why cowardly
leaders often seem overjoyed to point out how others acted
"inappropriately," or how someone else demonstrated "behavior that is not
consistent with the values of the department."

Such worn-out "apologies" just make it easier to identify the cowards who stand behind the scapegoating and the nonsense. But none of this helps. And blaming others and scapegoating has regrettably destroyed the careers of many dedicated, hardworking officers. The hardships these officers have suffered at the hands of cowards is enough to break even the strongest willed among us. Yet from a broader perspective, there's something even worse that happens. When cowardly leaders blame others, problems do not get fixed. In fact, problems tend to get worse—because cowardly police leaders are the problem. And by scapegoating and blaming others, cowards get away with it over and over again. Consequently, law enforcement agencies and the communities they serve get stuck in a vicious cycle of cowardly leadership and never-ending problems.

To break the cycle, it certainly helps to ask, "How did we get here?" And in seeking answers, it may help to think about one of the founding principles of modern-day policing "the police are the public, and the public are the police."[1] Somehow it seems that cowardly leaders have forgotten this principle, or along with their inflated egos, they think they're above everyone else—including the public and their fellow officers.

When cowardly leaders blame others, problems do not get solved—because cowardly leaders are the problem.

---

[1] Often attributed to Sir Robert Peele. See Thomas Svogun, *The Jurisprudence of Police: Toward a General Unified Theory of Law.* (New York: Palgrave Macmillan, 2013), 89.

With this principle in mind, obviously the public has every right to demand police accountability whenever problems arise. And here's the catch: if cowardly police leaders didn't cause so many problems—and fail to take responsibility—then the public outcry and demands for accountability wouldn't be so problematic.

Sure, blaming others or offering up a scapegoat may appease the public for the moment, but the real problems—the cowardly police leaders themselves—remain.[2] And when nothing really changes, and problems continue, the community gets more frustrated and demands more and more accountability. After a while, and rightly so, communities tend to lose faith and trust in law enforcement. And when this happens, disrespect and disregard for law enforcement festers, and the cycle of contempt, violence, and chaos keeps spinning round and round.

The "Out of Policy" Blame Game

Of course, cowardly leaders can't get away with scapegoating and lying to the public without justification. That's why cowards often use policies and directives to frame and blame. Just to clarify, that's *not* how policies and procedures should be used; they're meant to enable effective and efficient law enforcement and provide guidelines for clear decision-making throughout the ranks. Yet nowadays, cowardly leaders use policies to fabricate and justify "punishment for politics" and career-ending terminations, as though policies were guillotines.

---

[2] James Pilcher, Aaron Hegarty, et al., "Fired for a Felony, Again for Perjury. Meet the New Police Chief," *USA Today,* April 24, 2019.

In some law enforcement agencies, blame-game policies have become so absurd that practically no one could work an hour on duty without violating policy in one way or another. And many policies are written or administered by cowardly leaders who are so out of touch with the realities of police work that effective law enforcement seems like a distant afterthought. Unfortunately, there are plenty of blame-game policies out there. Although the following example not only points out a bad policy, it shows how cowardly leaders use policies *prima facie,* at face value, to play the blame game.

In 2015 and 2016, a series of officer-involved shooting incidents in San Francisco caused protests and political backlash. And just hours after one particular incident, Mayor Ed Lee stated "the facts are still emerging"—but nonetheless claimed that "these officer-involved shootings, justified or not, have forced our city to open its eyes to questions of when and how police use lethal force."[3] Granted, whenever "facts are still emerging" the best anyone can hope for is a get-lucky assumption. But let's pardon the mayor's assumptions for now.

If the shootings may have prompted "questions," it seems Mayor Lee already had the answers, although it took several months for the answers and the blame-game policies to show up. The chief of police resigned in May 2017. And by December, the San Francisco Police Commission approved a use-of-force policy that prohibited officers from shooting at moving vehicles.

---

[3] Emily Green, Bob Egelko, et al., "SFPD Chief Greg Suhr Resigns After Police Killing of Woman," *San Francisco Chronicle*, May 20, 2016.

The policy—a gift to car-jackers and criminals throughout the city limits—reads as follows:

> "An officer shall not discharge a firearm at the operator or occupant of a moving vehicle unless the operator or occupant poses an immediate threat of death or serious bodily injury to the public or an officer by means other than the vehicle."

The policy follows one of the 272 reforms recommended by U.S. Department of Justice. Obviously, the introduction of such a policy had a lot to do with hopping on the political bandwagon. However, the policy was also developed with help from the legal director of the American Civil Liberties Union of Northern California—who revealed some of the local politics behind it as well:

> "It's an important transformational document [...] I think that the Police Commission stayed the course and adopted a policy that fulfilled the mayor's promise to re-engineer use of force."[4]

Needless to say, San Francisco doesn't need a Police Commission that fulfills the mayor's "promise" more than it protects its officers. And law enforcement agencies do not need "transformational documents" or "re-engineering" by ambitious politicians that put the lives of police officers at risk. Instead, what's needed most are policies that promote effective crime-fighting and public safety—including the safety of officers—and not blame-game politics.

---

[4] Vivian Ho, "Police Commission Votes to Prohibit Shooting at Moving Vehicles," *San Francisco Chronicle,* December 21, 2016.

The policy itself says a lot about a lack of understanding of the dangerous situations that law enforcement professionals encounter, not to mention a lack of understanding about criminal behavior and deterrence. But how this policy has been used speaks volumes about how cowards play the blame-game.

After this misguided policy took effect, it was used to blame San Francisco Police Officer William Reininger in May 2018. After a burglary suspect rammed a police car, and drove toward another officer, Reininger fired two shots at the suspect's vehicle—with the intent to stop the suspect and save the other officer's life.

Ultimately, the suspect was charged with burglary and attempted murder. He was also charged with assault with a deadly weapon on an officer— ironically, the deadly weapon was the vehicle. Meanwhile, the SFPD homicide unit and internal affairs, along with the district attorney's office weren't even close to finishing their investigations—but that didn't stop practically every so-called leader from trying to dodge the controversies of the past, and pass the blame by quickly pointing out that Officer Reininger was "out of policy."

For example, in discussing Officer Reininger's case, Commissioner Petra DeJesus of the San Francisco Police Commission flatly stated, "The policy is very strict, you cannot shoot at a moving vehicle"—as though the specific circumstances of the case hardly mattered.[5] And mayoral candidate and president of the San Francisco Board of Supervisors, London Breed, (who later became mayor of San Francisco) was also quick to declare that Officer Reininger was "outside the policy."[6]

However, in courageously standing up to this absurd, blame-game policy, Tony Montoya, the president of the San Francisco Police Officers Association, had this to say:

> "We're sworn to protect the public and uphold the law. Just because we wear a uniform doesn't mean we should not be able to defend ourselves."[7]

Sadly, this isn't the only agency with misguided policies that prevent officers from protecting themselves. Blame-game policies are becoming increasingly problematic, especially when it comes to use of force. However, despite all the politics, a simple, yet profound truth remains: so long as the public demands protection from the worst of society, police officers must be able to defend themselves against the worst.

---

[5] Michael Barba, "Rookie SFPD Officer Shot at Moving Car in Apparent Policy Violation," *San Francisco Examiner,* May 22, 2018.

[6] Evan Sernoffsky, "San Francisco Officer's Shots at Moving Vehicle Rekindle Tense Debate," *San Francisco Chronicle*, May 22, 2018.

[7] (Sernoffsky 2018).

This isn't just rhetoric. If politicians and cowardly police leaders were less concerned passing the blame and more concerned with criminal behavior — and dare we even speak of deterrence or actually trying to prevent crime — they'd quickly realize that vehicles are in fact deadly weapons capable of killing people, including police officers. And they'd realize that even though it may be politically uncomfortable, there may be plenty of circumstances when an officer may need to shoot at a moving vehicle, or take some other action against policy to save themselves or others. And instead of paying attention to "politically correct" daydreams and delusions, they'd accept the chilling facts, for example, how four police officers were killed in the line of duty by assailants who used vehicles as a weapon in 2018.[8]

Here's another case that hopefully makes this point clear. The blame-game incident in San Francisco happened in May 2018. Several months later, a similar incident occurred in South Salt Lake (Utah). Officer Romrell, of the South Salt Lake Police Department, was responding to a burglary in November 2018. Tragically, Officer Romrell was deliberately struck and killed by a vehicle driven by a suspect fleeing the crime scene. Yet before he died, in his final act of his duty, Officer Romrell fired at the vehicle, along with another officer, and killed the driver. Indeed, Officer Romrell died heroically defending himself and trying to protect the lives of others. And yes, he shot at a moving vehicle.

---

[8] FBI Releases 2018 Statistics on Law Enforcement Officers Killed in the Line of Duty," FBI National Press Office, May 6, 2019; see also https://ucr.fbi.gov/leoka/2018

Yet unlike agencies plagued with dangerous policies, cowardly leaders, and blame-game politics, investigations into Officer Romrell's actions, including his decision to shoot at a moving vehicle, proved that he "did everything right."[9] So, there's an officer in San Francisco scapegoated for shooting at a moving vehicle, yet months later another officer in South Salt Lake is rightfully regarded as a hero for doing the same thing.

Apparently, there's a disconnect in the law enforcement profession. But it doesn't take a seasoned investigator to trace the source of the disconnect back to cowardly police leaders who use policies to pass the blame. After a series of scandals and officer-involved shootings in San Francisco, a slew of "reforms" were enacted in December 2016. The blame-game policy that prohibiting officers from shooting at moving vehicles was one of them. So the fact that Officer Reininger shot at a moving car in 2018, and practically every so-called leader quickly declared that he was out of policy, shouldn't seem surprising—cowardly leaders had nearly two years to practice playing the blame game for self-preservation.[10] However, the South Salt Lake Police Department did not endure the same scandals, or demands for the police chief's resignation and "reform" that occurred in San Francisco.

---

[9] Nicole Darrah, "Utah Police Officer, Marine Vet, Dies After Being Struck by Car; Burglary Suspect Killed." *Fox News.* November 25, 2018.

[10] For more on the subject, see Christopher Hood, *The Blame Game: Spin, Bureaucracy, and Self-Preservation in Government* (Princeton, New Jersey: Princeton University Press, 2011).

Granted, there will be times when policy violations demand discipline, which should be administered fairly and professionally. However, blame-game policies—and the unfair judgments of cowardly leaders that abuse them—should never be an acceptable excuse for the dangerous, if not deadly consequences they impose upon officers.

To sum it all up, when cowardly police leaders play the "out of policy" blame game, three things tend to happen:

1. cops lose while criminals win;
2. cowards continue to cause problems;
3. and communities suffer the consequences.

So, what can we do to stop cowards from blaming others and enacting blame-game policies? First of all, as Courageous Police Leaders, we need to join forces and fight back against cowardly leadership and blame-game policies. Granted, officers and deputies may not be able to directly influence a deputy chief or sheriff, especially in large agencies. And a rookie on probation is not in the best position to single-handedly take on the mayor or the town council.

But something can always be done to prevent cowards from winning the blame game. And we must do *something*, because every time a coward blames someone else, they get away with more and more. That's why Courageous Police Leaders must *wisely* stand up whenever cowards try to blame others. There are plenty of effective solutions, plenty of ways to work together, and plenty of ways to make our voices heard. But shutting up and "taking it" is precisely what cowardly leaders are counting on.

2. COWARDLY POLICE LEADERS ARE LAZY

"It's very easy to confuse activity with productivity."
—*Tim Ferriss*

Cowardly police leaders typically think they can do no wrong—but this assumes they would *actually* do something. As many of us know, that's not necessarily the case since cowardly leaders are typically quite lazy. Yet they put in a lot of effort to avoid doing work. And they're quite skilled at using all kinds of tricks to create the illusion that they're doing work, if not somehow working hard. For example, since leading, supervising, and effectively delegating require effort, cowards typically avoid all that and involve themselves in busywork instead. It may seem like work to anyone looking around, but much of their busywork is unnecessary.

Lazy cowards also seem to love busying themselves with committees, and strangely enough, "task forces." Serving on a committee or a task force normally requires effort. However, cowardly leaders often sit around in meetings and blend in with the crowd to hide their mediocrity and laziness. And since committees, bureaucracy, and consensus often take considerable time, if not more time than most people can imagine, it's the perfect pace for do-nothing cowardly leaders to make themselves seem busy and important. Yet they're not really fooling anyone, and not really doing much of anything, other than bare-minimum participation.

There's also all the petty mandates and directives that cowardly leaders seem to love. While these tend to do nothing to help actual law enforcement efforts, "*someone* has to do all the work" and monitor and control all the unimportant nonsense. And of course, there's nobody more qualified for such "responsibilities" other than the cowardly police leaders themselves. Of course, they'll also hide behind the illusion that if they're subordinates are running around dealing with petty mandates and protocols and appear busy and overworked, then of course, cowardly leaders must be working even harder to keep up with it all.

The cowards aren't fooling anyone. Aside from their tremendous efforts to hide their laziness by looking busy when they're not, there's a more important reason why cowards are lazy: laziness helps them avoid reality and progress, while keeping the status quo.

Lazy, cowardly leaders love the status quo
Sure, there's plenty of wisdom in the old saying "if it ain't broke, don't fix it." But when cowards uphold the status quo simply because they're lazy and too comfortable, it can cause all kinds of problems—which often negatively affect a lot of officers, in a lot of ways, for prolonged periods of time.

Speaking of time, thanks to lazy, cowardly leaders, there's plenty of truth in the jokes about the difference between "the business world" and the world of law enforcement. So, what's the difference between the business world and the world of law enforcement? It's about ten years. That is, status-quo police departments tend to lag 10 years behind the current trends and technology in the business world. Although in some departments with stubborn, lazy, status-quo loving leaders at the helm, 10 years is a very kind estimate.

Whether it's upgrading equipment, revising policies, or implementing better training programs, cowardly leaders seem to always drag their feet. And they'll gladly "kick the can" until the next meeting, the next budget cycle, or the next election if it helps them avoid doing work or making "tough" decisions.

For example, when it comes to upgrading and maintaining equipment, cowardly leaders are notoriously lazy. Every road deputy and beat cop knows that a police radio isn't just an electronic device—it's a lifeline. And sometimes it's the only thing that makes the difference between life and death. That's why it's baffling to see cowardly leaders avoid updating radio networks and equipment. It's inexcusable, plain and simple. But when the IT department needs to buy spare radio parts on eBay because the manufacturer stopped making spare parts years ago,[11] that should definitely serve as a wake-up call for lazy cowards who are daydreaming instead of doing what's absolutely necessary to keep officers safe.

When cowardly leaders are lazy about updating equipment or policies, or anything else that improves law enforcement efforts and keeps officers safe, it shouldn't be brushed off—their laziness should be considered a critical safety risk, because that's exactly what it is.

---

[11] Sam Morgen, "City Hopes Sales Tax Could Pay for Upgrade of Outdated Public Safety Radio System." *Government Technology*, August 1, 2018.

In addition to putting others at risk, when lazy cowards fail to rise up for challenges and change, they often hold others back from doing their best. This creates all kinds of problems, including ones that simmer for a long time, but then suddenly reach a boiling point. That's when lazy cowards scramble around actually trying to do something—not because they want to, but because they're forced to, or have nobody else to blame. This is how cowardly laziness suddenly creates "urgent" demands that typically lead to dangerous compromises, if not complete disasters, which will be blamed on others, of course.

Lazy, cowardly leaders make a mess of priorities

However, while cowards may be lazy, they tend to do a heck of a lot about things that are important to them. They'll loathe doing anything in general, yet they're fired up about their own "pet projects" and things that matter to them. This is one reason why we need to pay close attention to how the enemy thinks and "works." The things that cowardly leaders care about will typically get top priority. Meanwhile other more important projects and necessary priorities—including the ones that actually help officers and the communities they serve—will be neglected, if not ignored. And whenever this happens, and whenever we let cowards get away with it, real problems with real consequences pile up, along with tons of work for everybody else.

And what's the strange and twisted consequence of all this? Indeed, others get saddled with more work and more stress, while cowards get what they want without doing much. And cowards don't have to worry about upsetting the status-quo, because they're the gatekeepers of the status-quo whenever they're in charge of setting priorities.

Laziness: the cowardly act of sabotage

However, like a lot of things that cowards do, or don't do, there's a darker side of it all. And it seems a lot of people will do whatever it takes to scuttle or sabotage a project or an idea they don't like. And lazy cowards often use laziness as a form of sabotage. It's diabolically genius. Since cowards are lazy most of the time, it's hard to tell when they're being lazy, or deliberately stalling to sabotage efforts that they don't like. Indeed, if a project or a priority doesn't fit their agenda, cowardly leaders won't lift a finger. Or they'll find some excuse to scuttle or put off anything that needs to be done with the old "we don't have the resources for that" excuse. Which is just coward code for "I don't care."

And even when cowardly leaders are forced to take action, they'll find a way to avoid doing what's right—and will often use another favorite ploy: they'll put other lazy cowards in charge of "leading" a project, or assign tasks to those who are least likely to get anything done anytime soon. In so doing, lazy cowards are almost assured that things are bound for failure from the get-go. And they won't have to worry too much about any real progress being made. Of course, if things fail miserably, lazy cowards can blame someone else for it. It's a brilliant way for lazy cowards to win three times over:

1. nothing gets accomplished

2. cowards keep the status-quo

3. and cowards can blame the lack of progress on someone else.

Although not as obvious is another form of lazy coward sabotage: "the under-cutting trick." If cowards can't use excuses to avoid something, or get someone to lead a project to failure, they'll under-fund, under-staff, or under-whatever a project to make it fail.

For example, you can spot a lazy coward sabotaging a community outreach program when it requires several officers to succeed, but only one officer gets assigned. You can also spot it when a new public information plan might be fully staffed, but lazy cowards haven't provided training for the staff to succeed. And you can spot it when a crime detail needs three unmarked cars, but gets only one marked unit instead. The failure is built right in—and lazy cowards didn't have to do much to sabotage the success of others.

Indeed, there are plenty of ways that lazy, cowardly police leaders undermine the efforts of other dedicated, hard-working officers. To combat their laziness and the unfortunate consequences, we must pay close attention to what the lazy cowards are doing—and what they're not doing as well.

Cowardly leaders use laziness like a weapon—to keep the status quo and sabotage anything that doesn't fit their agenda.

Paying the Price of Pettiness

Several years ago, I was tasked with purchasing law enforcement driving simulators for my agency. It was a huge task, and cost taxpayers about $500,000. The team was doing an excellent job setting up the simulators, but I soon noticed that the hardware was superb, but the curriculum was far less than ideal. Fortunately, I found a company with a proven training curriculum that was willing to provide it free of charge. The only requirement was that I had to go to Salt Lake City to go through the training myself, to ensure I could train the other trainers and improve the chances of success.

I made plans to attend the training and put in a travel request for about $900 to travel to Salt Lake City to attend the training. However, I was shocked when a commander denied my request. The commander seemed to think that the simulators were a waste of time, and was apparently trying to sabotage the program. And denying the $900 travel request seemed to be part of the plan to scuttle the $500,000 investment.

Not being the kind of person to let cowards sabotage anything, let alone a training program that would benefit officers and the community, I made other plans. Granted, I had to pay my own way to Salt Lake City. But I was not going to let a cowardly police leader stand in the way of providing better training, no matter the cost, in money or effort. Indeed, there's often a price to be paid for being courageous. But no matter how petty the cowards may be, we can't let them win.

—Travis Yates

3. COWARDLY LEADERS SERVE THEMSELVES

> "Great achievement is usually born of great sacrifice,
> and is never the result of selfishness." —*Napoleon Hill*

When cowardly police leaders actually do something, it's usually to serve themselves. Sure, "to protect and to serve" may be a popular motto in the law enforcement profession. Although "protect your ass and serve yourself" is perhaps more accurately describes the ways cowardly leaders operate.

Indeed, self-servitude—that is, selfishly putting yourself ahead of others—is one of the most common, and most damaging traits among cowardly police leaders. Unfortunately, it probably doesn't take very long before a self-serving, cowardly police leader comes to mind, especially since the selfish behavior of cowardly leaders has proven disastrous for many law enforcement agencies. And consequently, it has left the communities they serve with problems they can only hope will soon be forgotten.

In serving themselves, cowardly police leaders create a wide range of problems from petty annoyances, to begrudging backstabbing, to destroying public trust. They've tarnished the reputation of law enforcement in so many regrettable ways by committing crimes, abusing authority, mistreating employees, conducting shoddy investigations, and even manipulating wrongful convictions.

Accepting bribes is perhaps the most obvious example of cowardly leaders serving themselves. Yet a bribe isn't just a bribe—it's a betrayal of public trust. So, when a deputy chief goes to jail for taking a $4,000 bribe,[12] it's not just an example of a cowardly leader being selfish, it's an example of a cowardly leader betraying the trust and hope of the community. And it isn't always about money per se. Cowardly leaders seem to love lavishing themselves in luxury. For example, some top-ranking, self-serving NYPD officials accepted all kinds of expensive gifts, including jewelry for the former NYPD inspector's wife, expensive hotel rooms in Rome and Chicago, and a trip to Las Vegas for the Super Bowl aboard a private jet with a prostitute on board.[13]

Unfortunately, self-serving leaders aren't just a problem for big departments in big cities. You can find them just about anywhere. And in smaller, more tight-knit communities, the consequences can seem even more damaging. For example, when a police chief took bribes for hiring a convicted felon on the police department, it took the small community by storm and left a lingering cloud of suspicion that may take generations to pass.[14]

---

[12] Tresa Baldas, "Ex-Detroit Deputy Police Chief Celia Washington Gets 1 Year in Prison for Bribery," *Detroit Free Press*, April 18, 2018.

[13] William K. Rashbaum, and Joseph Goldstein, "3 N.Y.P.D. Commanders Are Arrested in Vast Corruption Case," *The New York Times*, June 20, 2016.

[14] Rene Stutzman, and Kevin Connolly, "Former Longwood Police Chief Gets 4 Years in Bribery Case," *Orlando Sentinel*, February 29, 2016.

The self-servitude of cowardly leaders isn't always about taking bribes, or kickbacks. Sometimes the damage of self-servitude stems from privileges or even just attitudes, which doesn't do much for morale or inspiring others to fight crime. Needless to say, self-servitude certainly spreads contempt and distrust throughout the ranks. Yet sometimes the self-serving attitudes and privileges are so blatantly obvious, it's like they're hiding in plain sight and exempt from being called into question.

One of the most widespread, unwritten privilege in law enforcement is that the upper ranks *must* have the newest cars and the best equipment—even though they're typically the last ones to put such things to good use. And while self-serving cowardly leaders privilege themselves, others are often left struggling with battered equipment and broken-down cars and barely usable equipment. This isn't about "paying your dues"—this is how self-privilege gets in the way of effective law enforcement and successful crime-fighting efforts, while creating hazardous work conditions.

For example, officers with the New Haven (Connecticut) Police Department had to drive around in old, outdated, and over-used patrol cars that were so bad, some were actually falling apart.[15] We're talking holes in the floorboards, broken gas gauges, metal sticking out of the worn-out seats— vehicles that nobody in any "profession" should have to drive. Yet while officers were driving around in death-traps, four assistant chiefs enjoyed much newer, SUVs. And of course, the police chief had a brand-new SUV.

---

[15] Dave Collins, "Outdated, Broken Police Cruisers Frustrate Officers," *Claims Journal,* February 17, 2016.

This is just one example, and the bad examples of cowardly police leaders serving themselves are practically endless. But whenever cowardly police leaders serve themselves first, everyone else seems to end up last. Sure, they may embarrass themselves in the public limelight and get what they deserve. Yet whenever cowardly leaders serve themselves, others in their agency suffer—one way or the other. And the communities they serve end up paying the price for their selfishness in suffering compromised public safety, and having to bear the shame that selfish cowards often leave behind.

Beware of the many ways that cowards serve themselves—it could be their attitudes, or prejudices, or privileges just to name a few.

4. COWARDLY LEADERS
REFUSE TO LEARN FROM FAILURE

"Insanity is doing the same thing, over and over again,
but expecting different results." —*Rita Mae Brown*

If you're looking for proof that cowardly police leaders are insane, look no further. Indeed, the law enforcement profession is marked by heroic deeds as much as horrendous failures. That's why learning from mistakes is essential. Yet cowardly leaders rarely acknowledge mistakes. And they rarely try to learn from them, or use mistakes in any positive way. So, when cowardly leaders fail to learn from mistakes, and fail to help others learn from them, they're basically guaranteeing that mistakes are going to be made over and over again...

What cowards do not understand is that being wrong can help make things right—if not better. After all, being wrong is an important part of learning, and absolutely necessary for learning how to do things right.[16] When mistakes are openly acknowledged and reviewed in positive ways, they become sources of knowledge. And when mistakes are met with fair and predictable discipline when necessary, even serious mistakes can become sources of motivation—instead of reasons for cover-ups and misconduct.

---

[16] James H. McMillan, *Using Student's Assessment Mistakes and Learning Deficits to Enhance Motivation and Learning* (New York: Routledge, 2018).

There are plenty of books about failure and winning, and learning from mistakes, and there are plenty of anecdotes as well, including ones about how "failure is just taking a step closer to success." And we could examine thousands of problems in law enforcement that were caused by not learning from mistakes. Putting all that aside, perhaps the most important point to remember is this: when cowardly leaders fail to learn from mistakes, they're not just letting failure define them; they're permitting behavior that allows a tiny mistake to become a huge problem. And they're letting a single mistake transform into a pattern of failure—if not misconduct and corruption—which is the biggest lesson about mistakes that cowardly leaders have yet to learn.

Despite their promises, whenever cowards fail to learn from their mistakes, they can only guarantee failure.

A Lesson Learned...

I learned about "learning from failure" the hard way. Several years ago, as a new commander, I had to make a personnel change. Scott Walton was a 30-year veteran of the department and a great guy. But I felt a change could bring a fresh approach to the position. I had plenty of leeway to remove and re-assign anyone under my command—so long as it occurred during a certain month. It was, and still is, a management "rule" to not give officers a reason for their reassignment, to prevent any type of legal action or union involvement. "Tis The Season for No Reason," as it was known.

Scott was blindsided. And he wanted to know why he was being reassigned, as anybody would. I followed the "rules" and refused to give him a reason. So the short of it is, I turned a dedicated, veteran officer into a bitter, pissed off employee (for a short time). And I couldn't blame him. No one should be treated that way.

After six months, my conscious finally beat me up so bad, I couldn't take it anymore. I made a mistake and had to correct it. I called Scott and asked if he would meet with me. He agreed. And when Scott walked into my office, I looked him the eye—and apologized. I told him the truth. And explained why I had acted the way I did, and made no excuses for it.

While I asked Scott for understanding and forgiveness, I also insisted that he remember my mistake, so he wouldn't repeat it, if he were in my position someday. Looking back, it was an awful way to manage, let alone courageously lead. But it was a new role for me. And I was naïvely following my marching orders as expected—for which I paid a horrible price. This didn't affect my career—after all, I did what I was supposed to do. But I treated someone in a way that I knew was wrong. I did not treat Scott like I would want to be treated.

I am proud to say that since then, Scott has become an elected sheriff. And I'm honored to say that he was the first sheriff in America to require all of his supervisors and deputies to attend Courageous Police Leadership training. But most importantly, I'm grateful that he helped me learn a lesson, about learning from my mistakes.

—Travis Yates

5. COWARDLY LEADERS
DO NOT FOLLOW A MORAL COMPASS

"It's very hard to live with yourself
if you don't stick with your moral code." —*Jim Mattis*

Morals and ethics aren't popular topics these days. And depending upon which way the political winds are blowing, matters of morality can seem threatening, trivial, or taboo. But morality matters, and in the law enforcement profession, it's always mattered.

For example, morality matters long before the first day of the police academy. If morality didn't matter then there'd be no need to scrutinize police candidates during the hiring process. Background investigations, credit checks, interviews with neighbors and co-workers, drug tests, and polygraph examinations, would be pointless and unnecessary if morality didn't matter. Likewise, determining the "moral character" of a recruit wouldn't matter if it wasn't the basis for evaluating sound judgment and decision-making.

Of course, morality matters in law enforcement, no matter what popular opinion may be about the subject at any given moment. And it tends to matter even more as an officer rises through the ranks and assumes greater responsibility in police supervision and leadership. The public expects more from high-ranking leaders, and often expects nothing less than impeccable moral character and judgment.

So while there are plenty of reasons why having a good moral compass is important, cowardly leaders always seem to find a way to navigate around doing what's right. Or they'll jump ship anytime their morality is called into question. But that doesn't change the fact that whenever immoral, cowardly leaders lie, cheat, steal, or worse, they're disrespecting themselves, their peers, and the law enforcement profession as a whole.

Consequently, their behavior has forced us to change the rules, if you will. Most of us would agree that the first rule of law enforcement is something like, "Survive your shift and get home safe." But thanks to cowardly leaders and their lack of morals and ethics, a second rule seems to have become necessary: "Don't end up on social media." Indeed, being the source of ridicule is never a good thing. But the problems that immoral cowards can cause are a bit more complicated than that—if not ironic as well.

Without a doubt, social media has provided a way for many Americans to make themselves appear more (self-)righteous and virtuous, and separate themselves from unpopular immorality. And it's obvious that immoral cowards quickly become fodder for social media, bad publicity, and sensational headlines—which never help law enforcement in the court of public opinion.

But here's the thing, morals and ethics aren't just for "virtue signaling" on social media, or inspiring motivational posters (with or without cats). And they're not just boring topics taught at the police academy. Morals and ethics require action, as the phrases *"being* moral" and *"acting* ethically" suggest. Both of which require effort, which cowardly leaders seem eager to avoid.

Granted, nobody's perfect, and we all make mistakes. However, while most of us know the importance of being physically and mentally prepared for duty, it seems cowardly leaders have altogether forgotten about the importance of being *morally prepared for duty*. That is, they forget to prepare themselves for showing the moral and ethical conduct that people expect of law enforcement professionals—and the kind of leadership that law enforcement professionals expect as well.

Whether it's a momentary lapse in ethical judgment or moral concern, cowardly leaders have caused tremendous damage to the law enforcement profession. And some of the more shocking and disturbingly immoral acts committed by cowards have drawn the character and the competency of the profession into question—and who could blame the public for doing so? And that's perhaps the worst part about the immoral and unethical behavior of cowardly leaders. For example, there are no answers that can morally justify or ethically support a police chief who engages in a cover-up to hide police corruption.[17] And there's not much that can be said to uphold the character of a deputy chief that gets arrested for conspiracy to distribute heroin.[18] About the only thing good about such examples of extreme immorality is that they're quite rare. But that doesn't make such behavior any less sensational or problematic.

---

[17] Kyle Swenson, "A Scandal Sent a Long Island Police Chief to Prison. Now It's Brought Down the D.A., Too," *The Washington Post.* October 30, 2017.

[18] Pablo Lopez, "Keith Foster, Former Fresno Deputy Chief, Gets Four Years in Prison For Selling Drugs," *The Fresno Bee,* November 13, 2017.

However, cowardly leaders also engage in immoral and unethical behavior that is far more subtle, but nonetheless damaging. For example, cowardly leaders often avoid taking action because they're too lazy, even when they know it's the right thing to do. Or they'll avoid advocating against a decision because they're afraid to seem wrong in arguing against whatever seems popular. And they'll often fail to take a stand, and *stand by* instead while misinformation, rumors, or reforms run amok—because they've let chaos and confusion distort their understanding of right and wrong. Whenever these things happen, cowardly leaders are far from standing on the moral high ground—and they're far away from doing what's best for public safety and the law enforcement profession.

Cowardly police leaders lack a good moral compass, so be wary of the ways they navigate around doing what's right.

---

6. COWARDLY LEADERS DISCIPLINE INCONSISTENTLY

"The signature of mediocrity is chronic inconsistency."
—*James Collins*

Cowardly leaders often show their true colors whenever they discipline their subordinates. All too often, cowardly leaders dole out discipline that may be too harsh, too light, or wildly inconsistent. They rarely get it right. And instead of being consistently fair, cowardly leaders typically discipline according to their own agenda, whatever that happens to be at any given moment. And speaking of agendas, the discipline they prescribe often has more to do with their emotional reactions and fears, than providing helpful correction and guidance for future behavior, which is what discipline should do. If we take all this together, it seems the only thing consistent about the way cowardly leaders discipline is that it's consistently *inconsistent*, if not just plain irrational.

When cowardly leaders discipline inconsistently and irrationally, the lines between fair and consistent discipline will seem blurry, or non-existent. And without clear lines between acceptable and unacceptable conduct, and without ways for subordinates to challenge unfair discipline, the whole system of discipline becomes fair to no one.

Of course, this works to the coward's advantage. And they'll rarely, if ever, complain about a broken system of discipline. That's because they can exploit it, and use it to blame others and make examples out of them. It's also how cowards get away with going easy on their friends and allies—and lash out at others without any justification whatsoever.

Broken systems of discipline also help cowards to get others out of the way of their cowardly agendas. In fact, there's probably nothing better for cowardly police leaders than a broken, inconsistent discipline system. Which might help explain why some departments suffer so many problems with unfair discipline for so long.

Cowardly leaders skip discipline–and terminate

Inconsistency is a problem. But there's another problem that's been getting out of control as well. Instead of disciplining officers, cowardly leaders go straight to terminating them. While cowards let some officers off the hook, they're making others walk the plank. That is, instead of disciplining bad behavior, cowardly police leaders are just hyper-actively firing people for it.

Sometimes termination may very well be warranted. However, more and more people seem to be "outraged" and "offended" these days. And in the frenzy of crying out for "justice," it seems more and more people expect police officers to be fired for just about anything, according to whatever narratives or nonsense that may be "trending." The problem is that instead of responding to an officer's behavior, cowardly leaders are responding to the irrational cries for "justice" and firing officers—when discipline of some kind would more than suffice.

This should be deeply concerning, especially since cowardly police leaders seem to worry far too much about the number of times a video or image has been shared on social media, or the number of calls and emails they get about *perceived* police misconduct. And rather than explaining, clarifying, or standing up against the nonsense and chaos, it seems cowardly leaders have become overly concerned with "responding" to "outrage"—than making fair decisions about discipline. Just to be clear, the severity of punishment should never be determined by the number of YouTube views, Facebook shares, or Twitter re-tweets.

Terminating an officer when termination is due is one thing. However, bypassing discipline and terminating an officer has become a quick-fix for cowardly leaders to seem effective and responsible. Terminating an officer helps cowardly leaders avoid looking like they're too soft, or too slow in meeting demands for swift "justice." And politicians and government administrators also look good whenever they quickly terminate an officer whose been found guilty in the court of public opinion. Besides, quick terminations "give the people what they want" and can help quell political chaos. That is, until the next round of "injustice" pops up in the news or on social media.

Bypassing discipline—and going straight to termination—is the worst form of cowardly, inconsistent discipline there is. Yet most cowardly leaders don't seem to realize that by giving into the "outrage" and terminating officers, they're letting external irrationality determine internal discipline—and undermining the entire future of law enforcement.

And whenever cowards give into (social media) mob mentality and unjustly skip discipline and terminate an officer, they're also dooming themselves, even if they can't see that through the fog of their grand ambitions and lofty egos.

Absolutely, the consequences and fear of unfair discipline and unjust terminations are gutting the law enforcement profession—and causing it to rot from the inside out. For example, as a former lieutenant who suffered through an "appease the masses" firing at a state university, Stacy Ettel knows this first-hand, and he sums up the situation quite well:

> "We're all just the next call from being unemployed or indicted. They don't punish you with discipline anymore. They fire you, and indict you."[19]

Ettel is unfortunately just one of a growing number of law enforcement professionals who have suffered the skip-the-discipline treatment unjustly doled out by cowardly leaders. And that number is likely to continue considering a new "standard" for discipline that cowards seem to have adopted: the *appearance* of "unacceptable" behavior matters more than actual behavior.

For example, two Roswell (Georgia) police officers were terminated for supposedly using a "coin flip" app on a smartphone to decide whether to arrest someone for reckless driving.[20] A video taken from the bodycam of one

---

[19] Vicki Newman, "The Stacy Ettel Story," *Law Officer,* April 14, 2016.

[20] Tim Darnell, "Police Officers Who Flipped Coin to Determine Speeding Woman's Arrest Fired, "*USA Today,* July 27, 2018.

of the officers while sitting inside a patrol car, shows their lack of experience and perhaps their lack of empathy. That part is clear. And the video, which went "viral" and was popular for a fleeting moment, also shows the officers fumbling around with the circumstances of the traffic offense. That's when one of the officers jokingly takes out a smartphone and suggests using a "coin flip" app to decide the driver's fate—or so it seems. The officers picked a side and accordingly, the "coin flip" app indicated that the driver should be let go. However, the officers decided to make a legal arrest for reckless driving—they ignored the app and made their own decision. To be emphatically clear, the officers did the opposite of what the "coin flip" indicated; they made their own, contrary decision using their own judgment and acted upon it.

Ultimately, the driver's fate was not determined by a silly smartphone app. Nonetheless, that didn't prevent "outraged" citizens—particularly those who are easily influenced by social media and sensational news headlines—to mistakenly believe that a speeding driver was arrested based on a coin-toss.

In response to all the negative attention, and social media backlash, the chief of police said that he was "appalled that any law enforcement officer would trivialize the decision-making process of something as important as the arrest of a person."[21]

---

[21] Alex Horton and Eli Rosenberg, "Two Police Officers Flipped a Coin Before Deciding to Arrest a Driver. They've Been Fired," *The Washington Post,* July 27, 2018.

Could the officers have been more deliberate and decisive?

Of course.

Was this an example of police misconduct for which *the only remedy* was terminating the officers?

Of course not.

Regardless whether they should have been fired or not, their termination says a lot about how cowards handle discipline when they panic under public pressure. And whenever cowards panic, they're more likely to misinterpret facts, if not ignore them. Instead of making deliberate decisions, they tend to overreact, and do whatever it takes to appear "strong" in making the tough decision—even if their decisions are completely irrational.

It's difficult to ignore how these terminations seem over-reactive and overly political, as though they were fired to "show" strong leadership—which by the way, is often a clear indication of cowardly leadership. And this kind of cowardly leadership does nothing but feed the vicious cycle of the "I'm-offended-so-someone-must-be-fired" nonsense that has become strangely tolerated nowadays. Absolutely, cowardly police leaders who skip discipline and unfairly terminate subordinates are enabling an absurd dog-eat-dog vengeance that has gone way too far. And if anybody wants to know why officers throughout the nation are reluctant to be proactive and would rather stand down than stand up, it's because of cowardly leadership—and inconsistent and unfair discipline and the fear of unjust termination.

Cowardly police leaders play favorites...

While some cowardly leaders are too quick and too harsh with discipline, others are exactly the opposite. They play favorites and let some people get away with just about anything, as if though they could do no wrong. And sometimes they go after others for the slightest infraction with a vengeance.

In perhaps one of the worst examples of its kind, it seems Texas County (Missouri) Sheriff James Sigman was clearly playing favorites with Chief Deputy Jennifer Tomaszewski.[22] Whenever someone like Tomaszewski — that is, someone without *any* prior law enforcement experience — gets hired as a jailer, becomes the chief administrator of a 72-bed jail facility six months later, and then becomes chief deputy immediately after graduating the sheriff's academy, it's a pretty safe bet that favoritism is probably at work.

And wherever there's favoritism, you'll find inconsistent discipline, and that's what happened in this case. After inmates complained about mistreatment in the Texas County Jail, a local prosecutor called for an investigation. The Missouri State Highway Patrol trooper assigned to the investigation soon discovered all kinds of wrongdoings committed by Sheriff Sigman and Lieutenant Tomaszewski — who were ultimately both arrested for several felony charges.

---

[22] Joe Difazio, "Missouri Sheriff Arrested For Letting Love Interest Pretend to be a Cop, Bringing a Minor to Jail," *Newsweek*, July 20, 2018.

The national news headlines about their affair and misdeeds were bad enough. But underneath all the sensational headlines, and the troubling allegations, favoritism was also leading to inconsistently harsh and retaliatory discipline. Sheriff Sigman apparently let Tomaszewski get away with just about anything. Meanwhile, due to inconsistent and retaliatory discipline—or the fear and frustration of it—more than 40 employees were fired or resigned within a year. Needless to say, as this example shows, inconsistent and retaliatory discipline creates chaos and interferes with the actual mission of law enforcement.

Cowardly police leaders will exploit broken systems of discipline to make others look bad— and make themselves look good.

---

7. COWARDLY LEADERS AVOID CONFLICT

> "If you avoid conflict to keep the peace,
> you start a war inside yourself." —*Cheryl Richardson*

Law enforcement is a profession steeped in conflict. And resolving conflict is one of the most important duties of law enforcement. Yet cowardly police leaders seem to thrive in bureaucratic mediocrity—and tend to avoid conflicts big and small. And whenever significant leadership conflicts arise, cowardly leaders tend to bury their heads in the sand.

Sure, cowards can be vicious, and they'll kick and scream to get what they want. Although when it comes to resolving conflicts or sorting out controversies, they're typically nowhere in sight. That's partly because cowards avoid work. But it's also because they're afraid to end up on the "wrong" side, and miss out on praise and attention from those in higher positions.

Nonetheless, conflict is something that leaders *must* do. And truly courageous leaders often excel at predicting and preventing conflict long before there's even a chance of it. In contrast, when cowardly leaders avoid conflict, they create all kinds of unnecessary problems, and even more conflicts. And it creates a void in leadership that allows the "Ferguson effect,"[23] or the "nobody's got my back" phenomenon to creep in and take

---

[23] Jeff Roorda, *Ferghanistan: The War on Police* (St. Louis: JCR Strategic Consultants, 2015).

over—which has become an increasingly significant problem throughout the law enforcement profession.

Eugene O'Donnell, a former NYPD officer, and professor of law and police studies at John Jay College of Criminal Justice, tried to explain why cops across America are giving up—why they feel demotivated, if not paralyzed—and why many are just doing the bare minimum until their pensions kick in. O'Donnell makes several good observations, but perhaps this one says it all: "conflict is the quickest path to extinction."[24] That's because when so many cowards avoid conflict, and so many officers stand down, those who courageously stand up have targets on their backs.

Indeed, thanks to all the cowardly leaders, those who stand up to do what's right seem wrong—but the Courageous Police Leaders who stand up for what's right aren't wrong. And despite all the controversies, and whatever "reformers" and social-justice "warriors" want people to believe, the law enforcement profession isn't wrong either. Period.

This point cannot be stressed enough. Especially since cowards who avoid conflict have let "reformers" and social justice "warriors" get away with their greatest hoax: making the American public believe that law enforcement is wrong. Yet they've also managed to make law enforcement officers believe it as well.

---

[24] Eugene O'Donnell, "Why Cops Are Standing Down All Across America," *New York Post*, May 30, 2018.

Perhaps more than anything else, avoiding conflict is what makes cowardly leadership spread like a contagious disease. And once conflict avoidance becomes the norm, cowards get away with all kinds of behavior that nobody in their right mind would rationally tolerate otherwise. For example, some cowards avoid eye-contact. Some avoid answering emails. And some cowardly leaders take conflict avoidance to the extreme and won't even speak with their subordinates. All of which tends to leave officers feeling snubbed and disrespected.[25] Yet some cowardly leaders avoid speaking and interacting with officers because doing so would only make it too uncomfortable for cowards should they have to discipline or fire their subordinates, as some of the cowards have flatly admitted. Indeed, cowardly leaders are destroying morale 99 percent of the time—just to avoid a situation that may occur 1 percent of the time, if at all. Sure, there's something to be said for keeping "professional distance." But whenever exceptions and avoidance dictate the rules, things like cooperation and team-work barely stand a chance.

How avoiding external conflict causes internal problems

When cowardly police leaders avoid conflict among the ranks, and hide behind the chain-of-command for communication, they create all kinds of problems inside their agencies. And perhaps the worst happens when cowardly leaders avoid *external* conflicts and allow them to create *internal* problems.

---

[25] Michael Greenlar, "Inside Syracuse Police Union's Rift with New Chief: Elevator Snubs, Overtime, Respect," *The Post Standard,* March 21, 2019.

This is most obvious when cowardly leaders avoid conflict and welcome just about every reform, investigation, and probe for practically any reason, including just for the sake of keeping up "political appearances." Sometimes all the investigating may seem hard to believe. For example, the Portland (Oregon) Police Department opened an investigation about how it deals with homeless people.[26] A few weeks later, the chief of police opened another investigation concerning the department's use of force against protesters.[27] These investigations were to be conducted alongside other separate, independent investigations as well. If this sounds absurd, that's because it is. It's conflict avoidance disguised as "transparency" run amok.

Of course, transparency matters. But whenever law enforcement agencies become so involved with demonstrating transparency, and give into every demand for "accountability," and every so-called "probe," it becomes counter-productive to say the least. Part of this stems from the fact that cowardly leaders mistakenly believe that agreeing to everything and avoiding conflict is the easiest thing to do. Handling conflict can seem a bit counter-intuitive sometimes. And whenever cowardly leaders avoid conflict—the necessary, productive kind—they almost always create even more difficult and more challenging problems.

---

[26] Rebecca Woolington, "Police Oversight Agency to Investigate Portland Arrests of Homeless People," *The Oregonian*, July 10, 2018.

[27] Andrew Selsky, "Police Chief Orders Use of Force Review After Portland Protest," *Associated Press*, August 5, 2018.

Least of all, by giving into every demand for an investigation, probe, or task force, any law enforcement agency is going to run out of resources at some point. And if anyone is paying attention, cowards may soon find themselves having to explain why their departments spend more time and resources investigating themselves — than investigating crimes in the community. Indeed, a lot can be learned about conflict avoidance and cowardly leadership by comparing the time and resources spent on internal investigations with those spent on criminal investigations.

Finally, another problem caused by conflict avoidance that cowards hardly seem to understand is that when they automatically accept every demand for "justice," they're basically supporting accusations of wrongdoing and pulling a shroud of suspicion over their agency. This rarely helps morale, and it often disrupts productivity — and complicates making real progress.

But cowards aren't fooling anyone. While launching investigations may have become necessary for cowardly leaders to show off their accountability, true leadership comes from having the courage to make challenging decisions, and the courage to inspire others to follow you — not avoid you. So a lot can be learned about the cowardly enemy in paying attention to the ways they avoid conflict — which can help make it easier to anticipate how they will handle, or fail to handle important conflicts and decisions.

Comparing the resources spent on internal investigations — to criminal investigations — can be a good measure of cowardly leadership.

8. COWARDLY LEADERS TAKE CREDIT THEY DON'T DESERVE

> "No man will make a great leader who wants to do it all himself or get all the credit for doing it." — *Andrew Carnegie*

We all want and need recognition from time to time. And it's completely natural to want a pat on the back for a job well done, or recognition for hard-earned accomplishments. However, cowardly police leaders often demand recognition — when they hardly deserve it. And when they don't get it, or get enough of it, sometimes they'll just take it.

In our Courageous Police Leadership seminars, we ask participants if they know of any examples when cowardly leaders took the credit for something they didn't do. Every participant has a story to tell. Some have so many examples, they don't even know where to start. This says a lot about the state of leadership in the law enforcement profession. And it speaks volumes about how cowardly leaders take credit they hardly deserve.

But there's an interesting contrast worth noting: cowards often take the credit, while courageous police leaders tend to take the blame. Yet there's something more subtle going on: cowards tend to take credit for everything; but courageous leaders tend to take credit for *leading* — while passing the credit on to others. Indeed, unlike cowards, Courageous Police Leaders tend to limit the scope of things for which they deserve credit, and it typically revolves around their actual leadership abilities.

For example, in passing the credit and praise to detectives for arresting and convicting a murder suspect, New Orleans Superintendent of Police Shaun Ferguson explained:

> "What I can take credit for is taking individuals and bringing the best out of individuals and making them a team."[28]

Clearly, Superintendent Ferguson limited the scope of the credit he deserves to his leadership, which is something cowards rarely do. And in getting to know and better understand the number one enemy of law enforcement, it may also help to know that cowardly leaders tend to take credit for having outstanding leadership skills when they don't deserve it. So, if you can't stand up to a cowardly leader by directly taking their claims to task, questioning why they deserve credit for their so-called "leadership" may be just as useful.

It's also worth noting that when cowardly leaders take credit they don't deserve, it's often a distraction to hide or downplay other problems they may have caused, or other projects or initiatives they may have completely screwed up. With this in mind, it may be better to just avoid confronting a cowardly leader for taking credit they don't deserve. And instead, it may be wiser to seek out the other things they're not taking credit for or owning up to—and "flank" them instead.

---

[28] Matt Sledge and Ramon Antonio Vargas, "For Shaun Ferguson, a West Bank Police 'Brotherhood' Helped Drive His Rise to NOPD Chief," *The New Orleans Advocate,* February 1, 2019.

Of course, the best tactics for combating credit-stealing cowardly leaders depend upon the circumstances, the cowards involved, the ways they're trying to take credit—and the ways their trying to avoid other problems they may have caused. Although the most important thing is to recognize *when* and *how* cowards take credit they don't deserve—and do something about it.

Whenever cowardly leaders take credit from others, it's often a distraction to hide their weaknesses and other problems they've caused.

A Lesson Learned About Giving Due Credit

I enjoy giving credit to others, but that wasn't always the case. And it wasn't until I learned through embarrassment just how important giving credit can be. Several years ago, rookie officer Pete Maher had just finished training. Normally, when a rookie is summoned to the Commander's office, it's not for anything good. But I enjoyed meeting new officers and Officer Maher had something to offer— something that the community desperately needed.

Like many other cities, the downtown area that we served was being revitalized. And the crimes and criminals who had their run of the place were now interfering with people who were increasingly coming downtown to work, live, or enjoy the up-and-coming scene.

Officer Maher transferred from another department, where he played a key role in addressing similar problems. So I asked him to put together a proposal and provide research to help justify a special police unit dedicated to the downtown area, which is something I had been planning to implement for some time.

A week later, Officer Maher gave me a detailed report, with excellent examples, and sound research. I added a few other details here and there, and submitted the report to the Chief, hoping to finally get the project started. The proposal was accepted. And the Impact Unit quickly began to make a noticeable difference. I was proud of our accomplishments. But I wasn't proud that I forgot to mention that Officer Maher was behind the proposal.

As a Commander, I could put my name on anything, and take credit for just about any proposal. In this case, I didn't want to jeopardize the proposal by putting a "rookie's name" on it, in fear that the higher-ups would deny it without even reading it. Or at least, that's the justification—more like the excuse—I kept telling myself.

Ultimately, I realized that my mistake in not giving Officer Maher the credit he deserved could have negative consequences, like making him think twice about proposing good ideas ever again. Besides, it was because of his experience, his work, and his research that the proposal was accepted. To correct my mistake—and to give Officer Maher the credit he rightly deserved—I rescinded the original proposal, and re-submitted it, giving credit to Officer Maher who ultimately won an award for it. I have him to thank for not only an outstanding proposal that made a notable difference in the community, but also for teaching me a lesson about giving credit where credit is due. And reminding me about something that many Courageous Police Leaders know quite well: there's always a way to manage risks—and give others the credit they deserve.

—Travis Yates

9. COWARDLY LEADERS MICRO-MANAGE

> "It doesn't make sense to hire smart people and then
> tell them what to do: we hire smart people so
> they can tell us what to do." —Steve Jobs

Micro-managing is a particularly frustrating behavior of cowardly leaders. Of course, paying close attention to detail is critical in law enforcement. But that doesn't mean that everything should be put under a microscope and constantly over-analyzed, or that every single task requires dictator-like oversight. Yet when cowardly leaders micro-manage, they're not just killing morale and creating endless frustration—they're failing to do their jobs. That's because law enforcement needs supervisors and courageous leaders— not managers, and certainly not micro-managers.

Indeed, cowardly leaders fail to understand that *managing is not supervising.* And without getting into all kinds of leadership theory, perhaps the most important distinction to bear in mind is this: managers make decisions for others; and supervisors let others make decisions for themselves. So when cowardly leaders *manage* instead of *supervise,* they become decision-makers for their subordinates. Even worse, when they micro-manage, they're essentially doing everything themselves, while annoying everybody else involved. And it's especially troublesome when law enforcement agencies hire courageous men and women and trust them to make split-second decisions involving life and death, yet some cowardly police leaders don't trust their officers with the keys to the office-supply cabinet.

Bad management is one thing. But whenever cowardly leaders micro-manage, they become dictators, and trust, efficiency, cooperation, and good work go out the window. Since cowards typically don't have much else to work with, micro-managing becomes a way for them to feel powerful and a way for them to feed their egos as well. Indeed, all their petty demands have a lot to do with maintaining control—and avoiding the risks of being outdone. And since cowards fear losing power, micro-managing is a way for them to feel in control. And it's also a way for cowards to show their bosses how they have "everything under control."

Micromanagement is also a problem because it can be an effective short-term tactic—although cowards don't know when to stop. When they see results, they tend to stick with it, even far beyond the point when micro-management is no longer necessary, and then it becomes frustrating more than anything else.[29] And it's not just frustrating to the people they're micromanaging, other leaders find cowardly micromanagement bothersome, especially when it goes on for too long. [30]

From another angle, micro-managing may help cowards feel like they're in control, but it actually reveals their weakness and lack of control. And unfortunately, there are so many different micro-managing personality types that trying to discuss them could easily fill another book.

---

[29] Joseph A. Schafer, "The Ineffective Police Leader: Acts of Commission and Omission," *Journal of Criminal Justice* 38, no. 4 (July/August 2010): 737-746.

[30] Tracey Gove, "Micromanagement: Dealing with RED PEN Supervisors," *The Police Chief* 75, no. 8 (August 2008): 26-28, 30.

But generally speaking, it's a good idea to analyze how cowards micro-manage, and then challenge their micro-managing on professional terms. To be clear, this would be quite the opposite of bad-mouthing the cowards. Instead, pointing out how their micro-managing effects your decision-making skills, or how it undermines your sense of trust in their authority, or gets in the way of efficient operations could be good places to start, depending upon who and what you're up against.

And much like patrolling in the dark and shining a light on things lurking in the shadows, be careful when putting the spotlight on micro-managing cowards. Start with the smallest of the micro-managing details or tasks. Focus on them, own them, and use them to weaken the cowardly enemy step by step. In some cases, you may have to work twice as hard just for trying. But in other cases, you might gain their trust, and build genuine rapport, both of which can go a long way to putting a stop to all the micro-management craziness.

You're not alone—nobody likes micromanaging cowards. So, look around to find allies and wisely engage them against a common enemy.

---

10. COWARDLY POLICE LEADERS ARE HYPOCRITES

"Hypocrites get offended by the truth."
—*Jess C. Scott*

As we've pointed out so far, there are plenty of things that cowardly police leaders get wrong. And much like the never-ending ways they tend to micro-manage, there seems to be no limit on the hypocrisy of cowards. Without a doubt, dealing with cowards and their hypocrisy can be quite unsettling.

Unfortunately, it's not necessary to prove the hypocrisy of cowardly police leaders in this chapter. As law enforcement professionals, we suffer hypocrisy every day in some form or another. And as many of us know all too well, whenever cowardly leaders demand others to work harder, but do nothing themselves, they're being hypocrites. Whenever they dish out heavy-handed punishment for "bad behavior," yet demonstrate the same behavior, they're hypocrites. And whenever they maintain high expectations of others—but fail to meet the bare minimum of safety or ethics themselves—they're being hypocrites as well.

Indeed, the hypocrisy of cowardly police leaders can take on many forms and cause damage in so many ways. And the consequences of their hypocrisy extend far and wide beyond themselves, their departments, and throughout the profession—even though most cowardly leaders don't seem to understand that fact, especially those who are also blinded by their own arrogance.

Whenever cowardly police leaders act like hypocrites in front of the public, they make hypocrites out of the law enforcement profession as a whole. And the cowardly police leaders who lie, cheat, steal, and commit crimes are perhaps the worst hypocrites by far. But when cowardly hypocrites make news headlines or go viral on social media, they're not just damaging their own reputations, or the reputation of the law enforcement profession — they're putting officers at risk. That's because whenever cowards put their hypocrisy on display and make headlines, it undermines public trust. Consequently the public tends to become suspicious and angry with such hypocrisy — and rightly so. And who bears the brunt of the lack of trust, the suspicion, and the anger? A lot of times, it's the law enforcement officers who had nothing to do with such hypocrisy. They take the blame — along with the frustration and anger of the public as well.

And whenever law enforcement officers don't know if they can trust their leaders or don't know where they stand — while they're being held in contempt for the hypocrisy of cowards — it should hardly seem mysterious that officers avoid being proactive, or become defensive, or "look out for themselves," or even worse, become complacent. This is just one way how the headline-grabbing hypocrisy of cowardly police leaders is like a one-two punch that few agencies and communities can recover from quickly.

Without a doubt, cowardly leaders create all kinds of conflicts whenever they act like hypocrites, And the conflicts they create between themselves and their subordinate "followers" often lead to all kinds of chaos. Least of all, it makes officers hesitate, because rightly so, law enforcement professionals should think twice before choosing to "follow" cowards and hypocrites.

Furthermore, hypocrisy reveals a lack of integrity.[31] And in making excuses for themselves, and their lack of integrity, hypocritical cowards typically try to misidentify any conflicts that arise. For example, "personal grudges" or a "lack of morale" are two excuses that cowardly leaders often use to cover up their hypocrisy. But whatever the excuse, whenever cowards get away with being hypocrites, the consequences can seem overwhelming. Over time, it can create a looming problem that few people can pinpoint or identify precisely. And it typically doesn't take long for a "lack of morale"—a.k.a. the respectable unwillingness to follow hypocritical, dishonest, cowardly leaders who lack integrity—to become so pervasive that few can figure out where it's all coming from. This is just one reason why we must do better at combating the hypocrisy of cowards. We need to recognize it, better understand the consequences of it, and attack it like the dangerous threat it has become.

At its core, hypocrisy is a contradiction between what someone believes and what someone does. It's the rub between "do as I say, not as I do."[32] But hypocrisy also involves pretending to be someone you're not, or pretending to believe something you don't genuinely believe. From this perspective, if we consider the hypocrisy of cowardly police leaders and the hypocrisy of social justice "warriors," there are a lot of similarities between the two—and that should sound as alarming as it seems.

---

[31] Douglas Perez and Michael Barkhurst, *Paradoxes of Leadership in Police Management* (Clifton Park, NY: Delmar, Cengage Learning, 2011), 178.

[32] Quinn McCarthy, *Police Leadership: A Primer for the Individual and the Organization.* (New York: Palgrave Macmillan, 2012), 107.

There are many cowardly police leaders who will pretend to dismiss the ideas of social justice "warriors" and "crazy people with signs." Yet much like hypocrites, these same cowards will give into their demands, even if it means firing an officer, revising policies, or issuing directives that go against case law, common law enforcement practices, and common sense.

Likewise, hypocritical cowards say they respect their officers and will "watch their backs"—but turn around and use them for scapegoats without thinking twice. However, it's not just the actions of hypocritical cowardly leaders we need to be suspicious about—it's their ideas and their beliefs we need to keep a careful eye on as well.

In getting to know your enemy, the cowardly police leader, it is their hypocrisy that perhaps best reveals their true nature. Whenever a coward is being a hypocrite, they're not being honest with themselves. And they're sure as heck not going to be honest with you or anybody else for that matter, because hypocrites lack integrity. And it is in their lack of integrity, their hypocrisy, and their avoidance of reality that cowardly police leaders share so much in common with other enemies of law enforcement. At a time when American freedoms are under attack, when shame mobs on social media undermine free speech, and the fear of losing your job and your pension dictate how law enforcement officers think and act, we must absolutely take a courageous stand against hypocritical cowards.

So, let's not be hypocrites ourselves, and let's take a bit of our own advice. If citizens should follow the "if you see something, say something" idea, then we should too. And with that in mind, if you see hypocrisy, say something or do something about it. Do it wisely, cautiously, even ninja-like if need be. But don't ignore hypocrisy when you see it—that's what cowards are counting on. Besides, cowardly police leaders have been getting away with hypocrisy for far too long because we have yet to raise our collective voices and say something about it, and do something about it. It's time to join forces and be courageous, and send the cowards and the hypocrites running scared. Pointing out hypocrisy is a good place to start, especially since whenever people have a choice, instead of following frustrating, dishonest cowards, they tend to follow courageous leaders with integrity instead.

Will there be consequences and pushback for calling out the cowards for their hypocrisy? Absolutely. But the consequences will only get worse the longer we allow cowards to get away with being hypocrites, creating chaos, and spreading distrust everywhere—all while the public and the law enforcement profession suffer.

Cowards will get away with being hypocrites
—but only for as long as we let them.

AN OVERVIEW FOR MARCHING ONWARD

It goes without saying that the list of cowardly traits can go on and on. But hopefully, this "Top 10 List" offers some insight regarding the character of the number one enemy of law enforcement—and the nature of the problems they cause.

Much like the ancient wisdom of Sun Tzu's *Art of War*, the more you get to know the enemy, the more you learn about beating them at their own game. And if you know how cowardly leaders think and act, you can better resolve the problems they create, if not anticipate and prevent them in the first place.

Of course, cowards come in many colors and stripes. And they may be cowards in one way this week, and another next week. That's why it's essential to routinely observe what cowardly leaders do and how they operate—while paying close attention to the problems they cause.

To think you can beat your opponent or outsmart them—without really knowing them—is a fool's game indeed. So, avoid their cowardly traps while you gather information, develop strategic solutions—and most importantly, work with others to put an end to cowardly police leadership.

SOCIAL JUSTICE "WARRIORS"

"Love is blind." —Chaucer

If cowardly police leaders are the worst enemy *inside* a law enforcement agency, then social justice "warriors" are perhaps the worst enemy on the *outside*.[33] Their protests and demands for "justice" have taken a toll on the law enforcement profession. But their effectiveness has little to do with the fact that they're right. It has more to do with how well they spread myths and lies—and how easily they can manipulate cowardly police leaders.

Sure, social justice "warriors" and hypocritical activists may *appear* to have strength in numbers—that is, if the number of social media followers they have actually matters. But while they seem to have "influence," it just seems bigger than it really is—especially since it's based upon popularity from like-minded, misinformed, highly-distracted people on social media networks who often have no idea about law enforcement practices and public safety.

#SelfImportanceMatters
Indeed, many activists and social-justice "warriors" are self-righteous, self-absorbed, and just plain selfish, as evidenced by how much they promote themselves. And it's obvious when opportunities to discuss their causes seem to take a back seat to their own self-promotion.

---

[33] Quotation marks are used to identify something as questionable. And throughout this book, the term social justice "warrior" appears in quotes because they are hardly warriors in the true sense of the word—and the motives and intentions of social justice "warriors" are indeed questionable.

For example, the New York Times explains how:

> "some activists have been able to parlay their work into a level of celebrity—speaking tours, book deals, cozy relationships with politicians and Hollywood A-listers."[34]

And while their "causes" may matter, self-righteousness also seems to matter. Really good selfies matter. And clever social media hashtags seem to matter a whole lot too. By the way, if it seems like we're obsessing about selfies and social media—we're not. Much like magicians and modern-day snake oil "sales-persons," with a few pixel-perfect photos and a handful of social media hashtags, social justice "warriors" can amazingly transform a lie into a myth—and a myth into a "movement." And with their crafty social media skills, they can trick others into believing that what they have to offer actually works. However, while they may seem to be a formidable enemy, it's worth remembering that even the strongest of enemies have a weakness. And one of the many weakness of social justice "warriors" is that while they may seem to be out for "justice," they're out for themselves even more.

Many social justice "warriors" are trapped in (self-)identity politics. Which can help explain why they want to tell *their stories,* and tell *their narratives,* and attempt to re-tell history according to *their interpretations.* And the "warriors" with the bullhorns—the must-have accessory that they use to drown out other opinions and make sure *their message* is heard—are perhaps the most ridiculously obvious ones caught up in (self-)identity politics.

---

[34] John Eligon, "They Push. They Protest. And Many Activists, Privately, Suffer as a Result," *The New York Times*, March 26, 2016.

Indeed, this is a complicated enemy that seems far more interested in hearing themselves talk—than knowing what they're talking about. And they seem far more interested in shouting at law enforcement, than actually talking and trying to make real progress. In speaking *their* minds and telling *their* stories, social justice "warriors" are never wrong—the police are wrong. And thanks to all the socio-political nonsense that has engulfed the law enforcement profession, that's about all it takes to be "right" and self-righteous these days. Too bad it's become far more politically important to talk about problems than actually solve them these days. Which may also help explain how social justice "warriors" seem powerful when they're not.

Speaking of political nonsense and illusions, one thing that social justice "warriors" are quite good at is creating the illusions of "pressure" and "resistance"—two things that make cowardly leaders run scared. Clearly, social justice "warriors" tend to make problems worse due to their unwillingness to cooperate with law enforcement. And in taking a closer look, any power that social justice "warriors" have to wield doesn't come from *what they do*, it comes from *what law enforcement fails to do*.

For example, far too many law enforcement agencies fail to counter and check many of the absurd claims that social justice "warriors" often make. Sure, their demands for "justice" and reform may seem flatly asinine. But whenever we ignore them, and cowardly police leaders blindly give into their "demands," the reputation of law enforcement gets smeared across the nation. Subsequently, it's as though every department and everyone wearing the badge is to blame for accusations and exaggerations that often have little, if anything to do with actual facts and circumstances.

Adding to this mess, is the unfortunate fact that too many people tend to misjudge law enforcement in a matter of seconds. For some, their minds are already made up in the time it takes to pull out a smartphone and hit "record." And whenever social justice "warriors" hijack reality with *their* version of the story and the facts, they can triumph in the court of popular opinion, which is what social justice "warriors" seem to want the most—aside from being popular themselves, of course.

However, in getting to know the enemy, it's important to know *what* they do, but also *how* they do it. And it's important to know the strategies and tactics they use, even if it's only to steal their tactics and plays right out of their own playbook, or in this case, their "digital toolkits." Nowadays, it seems as though a social justice "movement" isn't a real movement without a "digital toolkit"—a collection of text, media, hashtags and other things that social justice "warriors" and their allies can use on social media to increase their popularity. And if you've ever wondered why a lot of their rhetoric sounds the same, that's because it is: a lot of social justice "warriors" are copying content from a digital toolkit and pasting it on Facebook, Twitter, and Instagram, and everywhere else on social media.

Of course, the "sample content" includes a list of preferred hashtags—along with requests for donations. It's all part of the self-righteousness, and part of their self-promotion. So, there's little reason to wonder that when social justice "warriors" look in the proverbial mirror—or perhaps look at their social media profiles—they seem to be in love with their cause, and in love with themselves. Which is understandable, considering how identity politics, and being the victim of something, are all the rage these days.

But as the old saying goes: "love is blind."

And just like being in love, sometimes social justice "warriors" and their allies blindly ignore the facts, evidence, and circumstances—and blindly conform to popular "movements" and myths. The "Hands Up Don't Shoot" movement is a perfect example of this. It was not based on evidence. It was not based upon objectivity. It was based upon misperceptions, myth-making, and flat out lies. Aside from their copy/past efforts, perhaps myth-making and re-Tweeting is what social-justice "warriors" and their allies do best. So it pays to understand *what they do* and *what they say* when it comes to self-promotion, myth-making and social media manipulation.

For example, let's look at how Jeffery Robinson, the Deputy Legal Director of the ACLU praised social justice "warriors" and the so-called leaders of their "movements." In stating his opinion in Newsweek magazine, Robinson praised these movements for "... forcing America to take a clear look at what we are really doing in the name of "policing" in black and brown communities." [35]

---

[35] Jeffrey Robinson, "Black Lives Matter is Still Here—and Avoiding the Mistakes of Their Predecessors," *Newsweek,* July 13, 2018.

Robinson continued:

> "Their public actions are visible. They were leaders in making sure
> that America knew the names Trayvon Martin, Tamir Rice, Tanisha
> Anderson, Mya Hall, Walter Scott, Sandra Bland. They have
> disrupted our everyday lives by making us focus on the everyday
> lives of people who live with policing based on pro-active racial
> profiling."

Let's stop right there.

It's really hard to talk about *civil liberties* when social justice "warriors" are
forcing America to do anything. And even if we can overlook the hypocrisy,
it's difficult to understand how such rhetoric isn't a disguise for making
myths. Granted, the ACLU does a lot of work that should be commended.
But if Robinson aimed to suggest that Americans must look more closely at
"policing" in "black and brown communities" — and that the people he
names are victims of "policing based on pro-active racial profiling" — then
such rhetoric falls apart. Here's the proof...

Sticking to the facts, Trayvon Martin was shot and killed by a civilian — not a
police officer. Law enforcement had nothing to do with the shooting of
Martin. And that's why it's challenging, if not impossible to understand how
this shooting involved "policing based on pro-active racial profiling" as
Robinson seems to suggest.

So how in the world does this unfortunate case have anything to do with law
enforcement?

It doesn't.

And that's why Robinson's suggestion is categorically false. However, that doesn't seem to matter because social justice "warriors" want us to believe otherwise. But let's not overlook the side-stepping of facts, and how emotional sympathy for Martin is pulled toward other incidents that actually involved law enforcement. It's a move that social justice "warriors" and their allies depend upon, because side-stepping facts to make sympathetic, more convenient associations makes myth-making a whole lot easier—and the lies somehow more believable.

If we continue to take Robinson's words to task, the unfortunate incident involving Tamir Rice was also not the result of "policing based on pro-active racial profiling." It was based on a 911 call and report that Rice was pointing a gun at a woman's face.[36] Police officers were not being pro-active; they were responding to a 911 call—and they inherited the circumstances, and had no say about who was involved or whatever race they may happened to be. Again, this suggestion is also categorically false.

The family of Tanisha Anderson also called 911. So, this unfortunate incident was likewise based on a 911 call—not "pro-active racial profiling." And once again, such a suggestion is categorically false.

---

[36] Evan MacDonald, "911 Caller Was Frightened Tamir Rice Might Shoot Him," *Cleveland.com.,* June 13, 2015.

Robinson also mentions Mya Hall, who drove a stolen vehicle into a restricted, high-security entrance at the National Security Agency (NSA).[37] Categorizing this incident as "policing based on pro-active racial profiling" is just flat out absurd, particularly considering how Hall drove to the restricted NSA entrance—and then drove at NSA security officers. Yet it's even more baffling to understand how protecting the security of the restricted headquarters of the National Security Agency at Fort Meade qualifies as "policing" in "black and brown communities" according to Robinson's suggestion. Which again, is categorically false in so many ways, and seems to be little more than a wild association at best.

Robinson also mentions Walter Scott, who was tragically shot and killed by a police officer. This is the *only* example that Robinson mentions that connects with "pro-active" policing. Yet while this association is both accurate and tragic, whether or not this stemmed solely from "racial profiling" remains questionable.

Lastly, Robinson mentions Sandra Bland who was stopped by a state trooper for a traffic violation. This certainly qualifies as "pro-active" policing. However, Bland regrettably died in a county jail from an apparent suicide— days after she was pulled over. So, it seems a rather dramatic oversimplification to say this tragedy was the direct result of "policing based on pro-active racial profiling," as Robinson seems to suggest.

---

[37] Tribune wire reports, "Driver Killed at NSA Identified as Transgender Sex Worker, Friend Says," *The Chicago Tribune*, April 1, 2015.

All in all, in praising social justice movements and their "leaders," the Deputy Legal Director of the ACLU refers to six cases, but only one of them directly relates to "pro-active" policing. So it should seem obvious how mixing and matching associations is part of the myth-making—which social justice "warriors" and their allies use to gain sympathy for their demands for "justice." And whenever facts are ignored for the sake of myths to "reform" law enforcement, we must absolutely question the social, political, and personal motives behind such myth-making. Unfortunately, however, cowardly leaders are too scared to question anything, least of all themselves.

That's not to say that law enforcement does everything right in every case. But as this brief analysis hopefully shows, social justice "warriors" and their allies often use confused associations and far-reaching narratives to create myths, including perhaps the biggest myth of them all: that law enforcement throughout the United States must be racially biased.

Unfortunately, the myths aren't going away and seem to be getting worse because cowardly leaders are falling for them over and over again. Sure, the claims of social justice "warriors" are absurd. But without a clear, unified response to them from law enforcement, the myths become even more powerful in misleading the American public and causing severe damage to the law enforcement profession. And that's what social justice "warriors" are counting on: they become more powerful whenever cowardly leaders run and hide, or sheepishly give into their demands—because it makes their myths seem more like the truth.

RISKING PUBLIC SAFETY FOR THE SAKE OF VANITY

There's a bigger problem, however. And that's because whenever social justice "warriors" and their allies fabricate myths, they're not just sending cowardly police leaders running scared—they're sweeping criminal behavior under the rug. And with this in mind, it's like the social justice "warriors" and their allies are trying to wield a double-edged sword against law enforcement: they're building up lies and myths—while downplaying criminal behavior.

If we briefly review Robinson's remarks, we can see how his opinion seems to involve building up myths, while downplaying criminal behavior at the same time. For example, Robinson mentioned the case of Tamir Rice—but he doesn't mention that Rice was "pulling a gun out of his pants and pointing it at people." And it seems the fact that someone called 911 out of fear because of the way Rice was behaving has been overlooked as well.

Robinson's opinion isn't the only one that overlooks or ignores such facts; plenty of "allies" of social "justice" movements also fail to mention that Rice had a replica of a real gun, and that the orange-safety ring around the muzzle had been removed making it nearly impossible to immediately tell it was a replica. And the fact that *Rice disobeyed lawful commands of police officers* isn't even a footnote in most of the social justice narratives about this case. The same can be said about the case of Mya Hall, whose criminal behavior involved driving a stolen vehicle at NSA security officers—in a dangerous situation that was solely created by Mya Hall.

We can go on and on, and examine plenty of other cases in which social justice "warriors" and their allies overlook criminal behavior—if not outright lie about it. And social justice "warriors" are absolutely lying by omission whenever they ignore criminal behavior and how it unnecessarily escalates a situation. They're also lying whenever they dismiss inconvenient facts and circumstances or "complicated" truths. Indeed, overlooking criminal behavior seems essential to their myth-making—and part of a broader effort of social justice "warriors" and their allies to condemn the police and drum up the biggest lawsuit settlements possible.

And here's something that social justice "warriors" and their allies also seem to have overlooked: whenever they ignore how criminal behavior contributes to a problem they are purportedly trying to solve, social justice "warriors" become part of the problem themselves. Ultimately, they're encouraging criminals—and discouraging law enforcement officers—and putting the public at risk with their myths and ignorance. This is why social justice "warriors" aren't just an enemy; they're part of the problem with crime and criminal behavior. Their demands for justice may help lawyers make more money, but they're helping criminals and hurting law enforcement—while disrupting and dividing America with their myths, lies, and deceptions.

Ignoring facts—and making sympathetic associations—helps social justice "warriors" and their allies create the illusion that law enforcement *must* be racially biased.

THE MYTH OF "SYSTEMATIC RACISM"

Indeed, there are plenty of myths and plenty of ignorance going around, but it seems like social justice "warriors" are beyond obsessed with the myth of "systematic racism" in the law enforcement profession. However, as former Milwaukee County Sheriff David Clarke explained, "systemic racism is so rare in America, the media just can't stop lying about it."[38]

And if it's not a myth or an outright lie, it's absolutely a gross exaggeration. Least of all, if something is "systematic," then it must involve an entire system. So if a law enforcement agency is "systematically racist" then *everything that law enforcement agency does,* and *everyone involved* must be racist. That means every officer, of every rank and every race, must discriminate according to the same racial bias. And the myth of systematic racism becomes even more absurd—and completely ridiculous—when it is applied to the entire law enforcement profession. Likewise, if the entire law enforcement profession was systematically racist, then *every officer*, in *every agency*, in *every community*—throughout *all of America*—must be racist. Never mind whether or not it's true, it's practically impossible.

But much like the way social justice "warriors" and their attorney allies like to make broad claims and apply them to specific cases, let's say for the sake of argument that the entire law enforcement profession is systematically racist. And let's assume that everywhere in America, every time a "white" law enforcement officer stops a "Black or African-American" motorist, it's

[38] David Clarke, "Systemic Racism is so Rare in America, the Media Just Can't Stop Lying About It," *The Hill,* November 13, 2017.

only because of racial bias. And let's just say every time an African-American cop stops a white motorist, it's *only because* of racial bias. Obviously, we're oversimplifying, and we'd need a matrix to include Asians, Native Americans, and other races to cover all the possibilities of racial bias—after all, that's what "systematic racism" would require to be true.

But even if *every* single "interracial" traffic stop in America was initiated *solely* because of racial bias, "systematic racism" still wouldn't exist. That's because social justice "warriors" and their allies are just cherry-picking one particular aspect of law enforcement to make a wide-sweeping claim and establish a broad-reaching myth. For example, much of their rhetoric focuses on traffic stops, which somehow seem to represent everything that law enforcement professionals do, according to them. Obviously, law enforcement involves a whole lot more, and officers would have to be racist in so many ways for "systematic racism" to be true, it's almost impossible to even imagine.

Like a lot of their rhetoric, the myth of "systematic racism" falls apart in seconds. If law enforcement is systematically racist, then where is the evidence to prove how officers are racist for saving someone's life? Where's the proof that officers are racist when they help people by providing directions? Where's the proof that K-9 officers (the dogs) are racist? And where's all the proof that bomb technicians are racist for dismantling explosive devices?

These questions may seem ridiculous, but not so much compared to the ridiculous claims of "systematic racism" that social justice "warriors" and their allies often claim. So let's cut through the nonsense, if racism and racial bias do not pervade the *entire system* of law enforcement, it's not "systematic." And if law enforcement officers are racist only when they write tickets or make arrests—and are not racist when they help people or save lives—then there's nothing systematic about it. Nevertheless, many social justice "warriors" have persuaded others to believe in their hogwash and hyperbole. And they've sent many cowardly police leaders running scared with nothing more than smoke and mirrors—and manipulation of facts. That's about the only "power" social justice "warriors" actually have.

Granted, social justice "warriors" may have legitimate concerns about cases of injustice. The shooting of Walter Scott in Charleston in April 2015 would be one of them. And the horrors that Kalief Browder suffered throughout the criminal justice system is undeniably another case.[39] However, not *every* interaction with law enforcement amounts to an "injustice." And that's the thing, when demands for "justice" and reform are made about practically everything, at the same fever pitch, it becomes unnecessarily difficult to collaborate with social justice "warriors" when it's truly warranted— presuming they actually want to cooperate, of course.

---

[39] See Jennifer Gonnerman, "Before the Law," *The New Yorker,* September 29, 2018. Also see Udi Ofer, "Kalief Browder's Tragic Death and the Criminal Injustice of Our Bail System,"*ACLU.org,* March 15, 2017.

But when it comes to crime, facts are facts. And it is criminal behavior that causes problems for law enforcement in the first place. Imagine how many tragic interactions with law enforcement could have been averted if people simply obeyed lawful commands. Speculation aside, however, myth-making strategies and tactics that downplay criminal behavior can help score points during a civil trial and substantially increase a settlement payout. And throwing in myths about systematic racism only seems to sweeten the deal. So despite the dire impact that all the myth-making and claims of "systematic racism" are having upon law enforcement and American society, it's unlikely that social justice "warriors" and their allies are going to abandon such strategies and tactics anytime soon—which makes it easier to analyze them, learn from them, and use them against the enemy themselves.

So let's not be confused; as long as the myth-making continues, the myths and chaos will continue as well. For example, social justice "warriors" and the media may have portrayed Michael Brown as a "gentle giant."[40] But a surveillance video shows Brown not so gently shoving a store employee into a food rack, and then intimidating him. Of course, nobody wants to remember a friend or family member as a criminal. But whenever social justice "warriors" and their allies downplay and dismiss facts and obvious criminal behavior, and toss in "systematic racism" myths, they're making excuses for the underlying issues beneath many of the crime problems in America—and using the law enforcement profession as a scapegoat.

---

[40] Elisa Crouch, "Michael Brown Remembered as a Gentle Giant," *St. Louis Post-Dispatch,* August 11, 2014.

Can conclusions about crime and socio-economic factors affecting American society be drawn along racial, cultural, or religious lines? Absolutely. But does this mean that every law enforcement agency in America is systematically racist or biased? Absolutely not. However, social justice movements would be a lot less (self-) important if things didn't appear that way. And belonging to a "movement" would hardly seem as necessary or attractive without self-important, bold-faced lies and myths.

If social justice "warriors" and their allies could put aside the myth-making, the ignorance of criminal behavior, and the accusations of "systematic racism," it would easier to address the more significant problems with crime and criminal behavior that we all need to address. But with all the myths, protests, and shout downs, and attempts to get attention for themselves and their causes, social justice "warriors" are taking attention away from the socio-economic problems related to crime that we should all be focusing on—and working together to solve.

Even more frustrating, as an enemy that uses various tactics to shout-down differences of opinion, social justice "warriors" rarely seem to listen. And many of the social justice "leaders" don't seem to have much of a plan for their "movements"—that is, beyond getting speaking gigs, book deals, and TV spots for themselves. That's why most social justice movements fail to actually accomplish much, unless we foolishly believe that getting cowardly police leaders to run and hide, or react with narrow-minded policy changes is an accomplishment. But it's not. It's just an illusion that social justice "warriors" are eager to show off as though they actually achieved something, when indeed, they have not.

And that's what makes social justice "warriors" such a problematic enemy of law enforcement. Their causes are often noble and necessary. But their strategies and tactics unnecessarily complicate any attempts to cooperate and work toward real progress, which ultimately hurt the causes they (purportedly) believe in. Absolutely, there are times to stand for liberty and justice, which is part of the foundation of the United States of America. Yet as history has proven, it is cooperation—not confrontation—that brings about understanding and mutual respect. As Dr. Martin Luther King Jr. said, "We may have all come on different ships, but we're in the same boat now." Ironically, many social justice "warriors" and their allies seem to have forgotten such wisdom.

But much like the way even a blind squirrel can find a nut, social justice "warriors" seem to have found a way to fool cowardly police leaders. Using myths and a lot of smoke and mirrors, social justice "warriors" have tricked cowardly police leaders into believing that their narratives and lies about "injustice" are true. And if that weren't bad enough, many cowardly leaders seem to believe the demands for "justice" and police reform are not only necessary, but urgent. But don't be fooled, the *strength* of social justice "warriors" is merely a reflection of the *weakness* of cowardly police leaders. Their strength is a mirage, especially since some cowardly leaders often become obsessed with appeasing the demands of social justice "warriors" no matter what it takes, or what kinds of reform they may demand. And it gets worse every time a cowardly leader falls for it—and every time a Courageous Police Leader fails to step in and put a stop to it.

"COP-BERATERS"

It's not a coincidence that standing beside the social justice "warriors," the "cop-beraters" can often be found. Cop-beraters are the ones screaming profanities or taunting law enforcement with all kinds of nonsense. And since cop-beraters typically feel as though they've been wronged by law enforcement, either directly or indirectly, or even just generally, they mistakenly believe they're entitled to do or say just about anything.

In many ways, cop-berating is nothing new. However, the defiance and the lawlessness associated with cop-berating has definitely escalated thanks to all the "right to be angry" opinions, and all the demands for "justice." And since cop-beraters often record or live-stream video of their antics to share on social media, they're influencing a much wider audience in their efforts to gain attention, notoriety, and "street cred."

Speaking of video, for many cop-beraters, standing up, mouthing off, and recording the cops seems to have something to do with a confused sense of duty—much like the "monitor the police" advice from watchdog groups like the ACLU. Indeed, the ACLU endorses such a strategy as part of their "Copwatch" program, which advocates "monitoring police conduct through personal observation, recording and publicizing incidents of abuse and harassment." And whether or not cop-beraters take their cues from such programs, it's hard to mistake their bizarre "civic" pride they often put on display while berating law enforcement officers.

Further, the ACLU claims such tactics are necessary to fight the "deeply entrenched problem of police misconduct" as part of a "well-organized, focused campaign against police abuse."[41] However, it's really hard to ignore the blatant hypocrisy—and how cop-beraters and social justice "warriors" are recording themselves blatantly abusing and harassing the police.

Of course, citizens have every right to monitor and record the police, and express their opinions, no matter how controversial they may seem. But cop-beraters hardly understand the differences between exercising their rights, disobeying lawful commands, and interfering and assaulting law enforcement. Some cop-beraters may very well be "doing nothing wrong." But their presence and their attitudes alone may very well incite others to act out in ways that are criminal and dangerous. And even if they had no intentions of inciting crimes or riots, or letting mob mentality run amok, sometimes that's precisely what cop-beraters and their influence seems to inspire.

For example, on June 9, 2018, a San Francisco PD officer shot a convicted felon who pulled out a gun during a foot pursuit. The suspect barely hit the ground as cop-beraters swarmed the officer. Never mind the idea that the suspect could have just robbed or raped someone (or that he was actually a convicted felon armed with a gun), the cop-beraters seemed unwilling to let reason stand in the way of their "duty" to berate the officer.

---

[41] American Civil Liberties Union. *Fighting Police Abuse: A Community Action Manual.* (1997).

The officer's body cam recorded the swarm of cop-beraters quickly spilling onto the sidewalk—smartphones in hand—recording the scene, and recording themselves yelling "F*ck you!" at the officer. The officer's body cam also recorded the angry cop-beraters as they became increasingly violent.[42] Several trampled over the crime scene to confront the officer—without much regard for the suspect who was shot on the ground. Meanwhile, the suspect's gun was still somewhere in the street. And it wasn't until backing officers arrived and began arresting the cop-beraters that the situation began to calm down. But it should be noted, that it was the cop-beraters—not the cops—who were escalating the situation, even though nobody seems interested in telling that part of the story.

While this incident shows just how self-absorbed and threatening and dangerous cop-beraters can be, many law enforcement agencies seem reluctant to do anything about it—in ways that are clear-cut and effective. Relatively few agencies are providing policies and protocols to address cop-beraters and the problems they cause. And for the most part, agencies that have addressed cop-beraters are only doing so after the fact, without adequate training and guidance for officers to recognize and address specific problems with cop-beraters and their criminal behavior. Yet even fewer agencies are enacting effective policies, providing adequate training, and addressing the underlying problems with cop-beraters, and the motivational or situational aspects of cop-berating behavior.

---

[42] Evan Sernoffsky, "Video Shows Police Chasing Man in North Beach, Outraged Witnesses After Shooting," *San Francisco Chronicle,* June 14, 2018.

Consequently, we have a kind of enemy that is undeterred for the most part, and this is partly what makes cop-beraters unique. Unlike most criminals who try to avoid attention, cop-beraters are likely to do the exact opposite. They're eager to make a scene because they're showing off and they want attention from people around them, or people on social media. This should highlight one of the peculiar characteristics of cop-beraters: they're not just spewing insults—they seem to believe that they're making a "statement" by berating law enforcement professionals. And like social justice "warriors," cop-beraters seem to believe that insulting or assaulting cops is their "duty," and necessary to support their own (self-)righteous ideologies.

Here's an example of the kind of things that happen when cop-berating and social "justice" ideologies overlap. It goes without saying that we should expect bold ideas and strong opinions to be voiced on a college campus. But when cop-beraters take over the swearing-in ceremony of a college police chief, while screaming "Death to Pigs!" and then steal all the donated food from the campus police office and vandalize a police car, indeed, rational behavior and critical thinking have left the campus. Unfortunately, that's exactly what happened at Evergreen State College, in Olympia, Washington on January 11, 2016.[43] And what should have been a peaceful, honorable moment became an opportunity for cop-beraters to try and make a "political statement" of some kind—and get away with criminal behavior.

------

[43] Jasmine Kozak-Gilroy, "Evergreen "Welcomes" New Chief of Police," *The Cooper Point Journal*, January 23, 2017.

Unfortunately, like many other cop-berating incidents gone wrong, not much was done in this case. That shouldn't seem surprising, especially since "shut up and take it" has become somewhat of the unwritten, de facto policy for dealing with cop-beraters. Compounding the problem, as though cop-beraters and cowards were in cahoots, cowardly police leaders seem to be doing nothing, or mistakenly believe that directives and memos will be enough to sort everything out, and make cop-beraters go away. But they don't, and cop-beraters don't seem to be going anywhere anytime soon. And like many other problems that cowardly leaders ignore, the problems with cop-beraters often go unchecked until they become so painfully acute or threatening, they simply cannot be ignored.

For example, it wasn't until after a growing number of cop-berating videos went viral on social media that the NYPD issued a policy memorandum regarding cop-beraters. But again, this was done *after* the videos became increasingly popular. The videos show the appalling disrespect of cop-beraters—and NYPD cops doing basically nothing about it. However, it wasn't until a belligerent cop-berater stormed into an NYPD precinct, cursed NYPD officers up and down, and caused a disturbance before strolling out of the precinct that finally some action was taken. [44]

NYPD Chief Terence Monahan condemned such disrespect for law enforcement. Ironically, Chief Monahan sent a video explaining the department's position regarding the cop-berating videos to the duty cellphones of the 36,000 members of the NYPD police force. We could dive

---

[44] Thomas Tracy, Graham Rayman, and Kerry Burke, "Cops Crack Down on Station House Videos After 28th Precinct Incident," *Daily News,* August 18, 2018.

into the particulars of Chief Monahan's message, but taken with the response to cop-berating from other leaders, here's the upshot: the disrespect cop-beraters show law enforcement professionals should be expected—and tolerated—because it's somehow been accepted as part of the "new normal" in the law enforcement profession.

But not so fast—by failing to stand up for the law enforcement profession, and the honor it truly deserves, and by giving in to every demand, every idea for reform, and every political whim, cowardly police leaders have helped create the social environment that has enabled and emboldened cop-beraters. And by not combating cop-beraters like the enemies they are—sorry, videos and memos aren't cutting it—cowardly leaders have allowed cop-beraters to become a common problem. And they've allowed cop-beraters to promote their propaganda with every cop-berating video they make and share—and use as inspiration to try and outdo one another.

And whenever cowardly leaders let the enemies of law enforcement go about their business of interfering with law enforcement and public safety, the enemies win, and officers lose. There's never been anything "normal" about such a predicament in the law enforcement profession, and there's no reason to let cop-beraters win the day, while law enforcement officers suffer the losses. In fact, the phrase "the new normal" is often just an excuse for describing how leaders have failed or have no idea to actually do something to combat an enemy or solve a problem.

For example, in speaking to the problems with cop-beraters mentioned earlier, Patrick Lynch, president of the Patrolmen's Benevolent Association made it quite clear that cop-berating videos prove just how hostile people have become—and how NYPD officers have become too afraid to take action even when they should. Likewise, Ed Mullins, president of the Sergeant Benevolent Association, said that NYPD officers "don't know where they stand," and how cowardly leadership has empowered this new breed of enemy:

> "We are being "led" by the wrong people whose policies are enacted for political expedience and police officers are regarded as collateral damage in their quest to enact progressive agendas.
>
> [...] Things are inherently wrong when society's miscreants are emboldened enough to verbally abuse and incite uniformed police officers, and believe it is okay to taunt them while 'armed' with cell phone cameras."[45]

As Mullins remarked, "the wrong people"—this includes cowardly police leaders—are to blame for helping cop-beraters become a rather unique enemy. The behavior of cop-beraters is blatantly obvious, but it's also blatantly criminal sometimes. And when cowardly police leaders are too scared to upset political agendas and let officers take action, cop-beraters are getting away with a whole lot more. Every time a cop gets put down, and cop-beraters get away with it, their agendas, ideologies, and demands for "justice" become more powerful—no matter how absolutely ridiculous they may be. Which only helps make cop-berating become more "popular" and somehow more necessary.

---

[45] NYPD Sergeants Benevolent Association's, *The Ferguson Effect in the NYPD*, Facebook.com,., August 15, 2018. https://www.facebook.com/sbanypd/

Cop-beraters, like any other enemy of law enforcement, should not be ignored. But if you don't have the support you need to take action, or are left without solid ground to stand on, sometimes it's wise to avoid combat until circumstances are more favorable, and the outcome more predictable. Indeed, in waging warfare, patience can pay huge dividends. And sometimes it's best to let the enemy "win" the battle—so they can lose the war. This may seem a bit counterintuitive. However, a case involving teenage brothers who berated NYPD cops in a stairwell should clear up any doubt about the effectiveness of this theory and approach.[46]

On August 8, 2018, Rockeem and Raquan McMillian, berated NYPD officers as they were leaving the building where the two brothers lived. The video of their insults should offend anyone in the law enforcement profession—but the officers did nothing and ultimately left. And it would seem that cop-beraters won the day. However, about two weeks later, Rockeem was arrested for robbery, and his brother Raquan was arrested for committing another separate robbery around the same time. If that wasn't enough of a coincidence, they were both quickly identified as robbery suspects—because of the cop-berating video they made. Granted, not every encounter with cop-beraters will end with such poetic justice.

So let's be clear: cop-beraters are an enemy that should not be tolerated or ignored. And the typical behaviors of cop-beraters—and what's legal and illegal for them to do—should be precisely spelled out so officers know where they stand. Likewise, any policies and directives that may be

---

[46] Tina Moore, "Teens Caught on Video Insulting Cops Busted for Robberies," *New York Post*, August 22, 2018.

necessary should be made absolutely crystal clear. It may also be a good idea to work with local prosecutors to clear up any confusion about how cases involving cop-beraters will be prosecuted. And of course, officers should be given plenty of training in recognizing and dealing with cop-beraters. They should almost instinctively know precisely when and how cop-beraters cross the line between rightfully exercising free speech and recording the police— and when they're committing a crime. Because quite regrettably, thanks to cowardly leadership, it doesn't seem like cop-beraters are going to disappear anytime soon.

THE ENEMY OF YOUR ENEMY

"The enemy of my enemy is my friend"
—Ancient Indian proverb

Whether it's cowardly police leaders, social justice "warriors," or cop-beraters, law enforcement has plenty of enemies. And knowing who they are and how they operate is absolutely critical. But it's also worth keeping in mind that the enemy of your enemy can be a powerful ally in the fight against crime, criminals, and chaos.

No matter where you go, every village has its crook. But while there's some who do wrong, there are plenty who do right. And thankfully there are also some people who care so much about their community that they'll do everything they can to help make things better. These are the kind of community leaders, activists, and change-agents we should be willing to embrace.

Granted, some so-called community leaders and activists may be as confused, conceited, and corrupted as can be. But don't be too quick to dismiss them all. Some are just as tired and fed up with all the crime, chaos, and cowardly leadership—which in a sense, makes them allies. And anyone who considers criminals, cowardly leaders, social justice "warriors," and cop-beraters to be enemies, is indeed an ally and a friend of law enforcement.

Of course, we're not talking about the "hired" organizers with social media savvy who can get people with signs to show up whenever law enforcement "controversy" arises, even if it's not where they actually live. We're talking about the community leaders and activists with genuine concern, who demonstrate sincere leadership and remarkable intuition. We're talking about the ones who are courageous enough to work with law enforcement—the ones who are enemies of the enemies of law enforcement, and therefore, should be considered our friends and allies.

For example, consider activist Demetrius Nash (D.Nash). In response to the police shooting of Harith "Snoop" Augustus in July 2018, Nash demonstrated tremendous courage toward helping his community. He condemned the shooting, but also "cautioned community members not to take up battles on behalf of people breaking the law." [47] He insisted that, "If the community is in an uproar, we have to make sure it's about a righteous cause."

Nash was talking about things that enemies of law enforcement often ignore. And he also took a realistic approach toward our circumstances—something that plenty of enemies with harebrained ideologies refuse to accept. Yet perhaps most importantly, Nash reminded others about the necessity of working together: "We're not going to get rid of the police, we're not going to get rid of the community, we've got to find a way to live together."

---

[47] William Lee, "As Unrest Follows Latest Chicago Police Shooting, Neighbors and Activists Plot Ways to Unify Their Community," *Chicago Tribune*, July 18, 2018.

And "working together" as Nash put it, requires genuine cooperation and mutual respect, which can make a big difference in dealing with the true enemies and the real problems that both cops and communities share.

Indeed, community leaders and activists can be strong allies. However, in many ways, the greatest allies of law enforcement, are members of the community—the people we are sworn to protect and serve. Of course, whenever you mention the word "community," the idea of "community policing" tends to follow. And like so many other things, cowards tend to take the wrong approach toward community policing as well—and they overlook how the community can be a tremendous ally of law enforcement.

For one thing, community policing is hardly anything new. It dates back to 1829, when the Metropolitan Police in London was founded by Sir Robert Peel. Along with the first joint commissioners of the Metro Police, Peel made sure that several principles were issued to every officer to help guide them in their duties. Despite the centuries that have passed, many officers still consult "Peel's Principles." For example, former NYPD Police Commissioner William J. Bratton remarked, "I carry these with me everywhere. My bible."[48]

And with regard to "community policing," four of the nine principles speak to the importance of strong relationships between the police and the public. However, perhaps principle #7 sums up "community policing" quite succinctly—and explains a key point that cowards often forget:

---

[48] Joseph Goldstein and J. David Goodman, "A London Guide for 1 Police Plaza," *The New York Times,* April 15, 2014.

"Police, at all times, should maintain a relationship with the public that gives reality to the historic tradition that the police are the public and the public are the police; the police being only members of the public who are paid to give full-time attention to duties which are incumbent on every citizen in the interests of community welfare."[49]

Notice that principle mentions "maintaining a relationship with the public"—not "serving" the public. Citizens aren't "customers," and cops aren't "customer service representatives" strictly speaking. Instead it makes it clear how the police are "members of the public" who are "paid" to pay attention to the duties "incumbent on every citizen." In other words, every citizen has a duty to stand up to criminals and protect their community from crime. So yes, the police and the public are an allied force with common duties, and a common enemy—criminals.

But as usual, cowardly police leaders are only making a mess of things. And they seem completely confused about community policing. Community policing isn't about *serving* the community. It's not about *working for* the community. And it's not about *giving back* to the community. It's about *working in* the community. And when law enforcement agencies adopt the mindset that the police are part of the community—and part of an allied force with common enemies—that's when truly effective community policing begins. And that's when cowards, chaos, and crime don't stand a chance.

---

[49] Thomas Svogun, *The Jurisprudence of Police: Toward a General Unified Theory of Law.* (New York: Palgrave Macmillan, 2013), 89.

PART II

KNOW

YOURSELF

KNOW WHAT IT TAKES TO
BE A COURAGEOUS LEADER

"Courage is the first virtue...
it makes all the other virtues possible" — Aristotle

In following the wisdom of Sun Tzu, you should know your enemies. And you should also know yourself—including your limitations, your strengths, and your weaknesses—and what it takes to be a Courageous Police Leader. Of course, it's easy to say that a Courageous Police Leader is the opposite of a cowardly leader, but there's a bit more to it than that.

Perhaps first and foremost, being a Courageous Police Leader involves a commitment to a code of honor—and a commitment to not letting the cowards win. It's also about being committed to courageously doing the right thing, even if it demands tremendous personal sacrifice. There's more theory involved of course, but essentially, we can see courageous leadership in practice whenever we find Courageous Police Leaders demonstrating these "Top 10" characteristics.

While many other characteristics may come to mind, these "Top 10" are some of the things that many Courageous Police Leaders have in common, especially when it comes to facing controversy and confronting adversity.

TOP 10 CHARACTERISTICS OF COURAGEOUS POLICE LEADERS

Courageous Police Leaders...

1. serve others first.

2. follow the "police like you want to be policed" rule.

3. build trust.

4. respond instead of react.

5. accept accountability—and challenge assumptions.

6. anticipate chaos.

7. listen and learn.

8. lead by example.

9. tell the truth.

10. stay in the fight.

1. COURAGEOUS POLICE LEADERS
SERVE OTHERS FIRST

"Everybody can be great… because anybody can serve."
—*Martin Luther King Jr.*

If there's one thing that truly sets Courageous Police Leaders apart, it's the way they serve others before serving themselves. They selflessly make tremendous sacrifices, even when there isn't anybody around to notice. And they serve others not only when it's convenient or popular, or when it suits their own agenda, but whenever it's necessary—and in ways that cowards would hardly ever think about.

By putting others first, Courageous Police Leaders demonstrate their responsibility as a leader—and why others should follow them. Which is tremendously important because great leaders need great followers. And as many Courageous Police Leaders know, their success depends upon those who follow.

It's easy to be a coward and demand that others follow you, or force them into compromising situations where they have little if any choice. But it's a lot harder to be a strong leader, who others want to follow—which has a lot to do with courage and the willingness to serve others first.

For example, Gary (Indiana) Police Chief Richard Allen made it very clear when he became chief, that instead of just talking about "community policing," he was going to do what it takes to make it work. Which for Chief Allen meant working hard to give his officers the training, tools, and supervision they need to build trust, and earn the respect of citizens. As the top-ranking leader, Chief Allen acknowledged that he and others in the top ranks "make decisions." But he understood how good decisions support the efforts of the officers, "the ones doing all the legwork." And he made it very clear that he expects leaders to do whatever it takes so that officers can succeed. But perhaps the most important thing Chief Allen did, was to recognize that his success depends upon the success of his officers and their efforts. If you don't think Chief Allen's approach isn't a courageous shift in leadership, just think about how many police leaders lead with his approach:

> "Every once in a while you get that sense of accomplishment or someone comes up and thanks you for what you did... And that's what I want the patrol officers to have, that sense of accomplishment, that sense of job satisfaction."[1]

Without a doubt, if more police leaders acknowledged how their success depends on the success of others, and focused on contributing to their sense of accomplishment and job satisfaction, indeed, the law enforcement profession would be in a much different state than it is today. Least of all, it would once again be a highly respected profession that people would flock to, instead of avoid and disrespect.

Likewise, Kennewick (Maine) Police Chief Ken Hohenberg understands why leaders must serve their followers. Chief Hohenberg understands that serving others is not a sign of weakness, but a sign of truly courageous leadership and great strength. Chief Hohenberg explains, "I go to work

---

[1] Becky Jacobs, "New Gary Police Chief Says He Will Judge His Success by His Officers." *Chicago Tribune,* February 2, 2018.

every day realizing that my job is to support the people who work for the Kennewick Police Department."[2] Notice how he sees it as *his job*, to support and serve others—not the other way around, which is what plenty of cowardly leaders mistakenly believe.

Courageous Police Leaders like Chief Allen and Chief Hohenberg recognize that the true measure of their leadership depends upon others and how well they can perform their jobs. Yet perhaps more importantly, in serving others first, Allen, Hohenberg, and other leaders like them also understand how serving others helps build trust—the contagious kind. The kind of trust that you can sense when you walk into an agency, or instantly recognize when officers interact with each other on patrol. It's the kind of trust that flows out into the communities they serve—and flows back to the department as well. Indeed, unstoppable crime fighting efforts, and outstanding community relationships often start with courageous leaders who serve others first, which forms a strong sense of trust and understanding in their departments, and ultimately within the community.

This isn't just about leadership nonsense and feel-good deeds. There are real benefits to having humble leaders and building genuine trust. Least of all, while every law enforcement agency faces some kind of crime challenge, when leaders serve others first, there tends to be a whole lot less chaos in the community. And officers can get the job done, with less work, and less hassle for the most part.

---

[2] Cameron Probert, "This Longtime Kennewick Cop is a Model for Police Chiefs. He's Celebrating 40 Years on the Job," *Tri-City Herald*, July 17, 2018.

For example, when Courageous Police Leaders are out serving the public—as though the public truly matters most—people tend to notice. This helps cut down the "barriers" that typically complicate cowardly leadership. It also helps people feel less afraid of law enforcement, and more willing to help, whether as volunteers, being a witness, or just helping by reporting a crime. Of course, in high-crime areas people are reluctant to be mistaken for a snitch. But when citizens know that police leaders and police officers are genuinely trying to serve others, they tend to find some way to reach out on the proverbial "down low."

When people know that law enforcement agencies care and make good-faith efforts to serve others first, even their crime scenes look different. Instead of walls of protestors and shouting cop-beraters, these agencies often have people lined up eager to help, instead of trying to harm law enforcement. But none of this is possible without Courageous Police Leaders who are willing to serve others first. And it starts with assuming the responsibility and the duty to serve others, and courageously leading by putting followers first.

2. COURAGEOUS POLICE LEADERS FOLLOW THE "POLICE LIKE YOU WANT TO BE POLICED" RULE

"Goodness is about character—integrity, honesty, kindness, generosity, moral courage, and the like. More than anything else, it is about how we treat other people." —Dennis Prager

There's a lot to the old saying, "your badge gives you authority, but your behavior grants you respect." And when it comes to gaining respect in law enforcement, and showing respect for others, there is perhaps no other rule worth following than this: "police like you want to be policed."

Courageous Police Leaders not only understand this principle, they live by it. And they know that putting these seven words into action can help them earn respect and dignity from their peers and the public—and help spare them from a lot of embarrassment throughout their careers.

Courageous Police Leaders also recognize the importance of this rule and embody it. They don't put on their badge without reminding themselves about it. And they don't get out of a patrol car, or stand up from their desk without keeping this rule in mind—if it's just ingrained in the back of their minds. However, as Courageous Police Leaders so often do, they put words into action, and they "police like they want to be policed."

Seven Words Every Cop Must Know...

My father was a former college athlete, Marine, Vietnam veteran and a police officer. So as a kid, I didn't need to go to the movies and watch Superman or Batman—I could just go home and see my dad. He was my hero and I was very proud to grow up in a law enforcement family.

My dad rarely spoke about Vietnam or being a police officer, and was mostly quiet and humble. When I got older, I headed off to college to pursue what I thought would be a career in athletics and coaching. But all that changed when I was 19 and went on a police ride-along. It changed my life. And I never looked back.

I started out as a cadet in Fort Smith, Arkansas washing police cars and running the chief's uniforms back and forth to the dry cleaner. I guess it would be hard to imagine more humble beginnings of a law enforcement career, except for maybe cleaning out the horse stalls for the mounted patrol. But I loved every minute of it.

I was excited to be a part of the law enforcement profession, and proud to follow in my dad's footsteps. And I expected that at some point, my dad would sit me down and impart some sage wisdom about police work. I thought that with each new skill or lesson learned in the academy, he'd explain what it was really all about. I kept waiting for the moment... But he didn't say a word.

So on graduation day, after finishing the police academy, I thought for sure my dad would finally share all the wisdom he'd been holding back. I mean, of course he would be obligated to say something, at the proud moment when a police father pins a badge on his police son. Finally, he spoke and imparted his wisdom about policing: "Treat others like you want to be treated."

I thought to myself, "Heck, is that it? I learned that in kindergarten!"

I thought for sure there was more to being a cop, after all I didn't exactly see that in cop TV shows or movies. And my dad was a cop since I could remember—certainly he must've experienced much more and had more to say than that.

It would take years before I eventually realized the tremendous power of those words. As it turns out, my dad was right. And it was precisely because of his years of hard work, and his experience rising through the ranks that he was able to condense much-needed advice into hardly a sentence. And if there's one thing you can take away from this book, any one thing that you get out of Courageous Police Leadership, let it be this: *"Police like you want to be policed."* Or as a great man once told me, "Treat others like you want to be treated."

—Travis Yates

3. COURAGEOUS POLICE LEADERS BUILD TRUST

"Trust is the glue that holds people together and is the lubricant that keeps an organization moving forward." — *Colin Powell*

If you can do nothing else but "serve others first" and "police like you want to be policed," you'll be doing something that thousands of cowardly police leaders never achieve no matter how hard they try: they build trust — and trust makes all the difference.

When Courageous Police Leaders build trust, they inspire those around them. When they build trust, they can delegate and get more done because they can trust others to do their jobs. And when Courageous Police Leaders build trust, they can drastically reduce the need for lies, the need for misconduct, and a host of all other kinds of problems that tend to follow cowardly leaders around — including the problems that tend to engulf law enforcement agencies in chaos.

In contrast, the problems that plague most dysfunctional agencies often trace back to cowardly leaders who don't trust anyone, even with the small stuff. There's no excuse for being a control freak. And this kind of "leadership" doesn't build trust — it builds resentment. Fortunately, Courageous Police Leaders know better. They understand that their greatest assets are the people around them. And they understand that they must build trust by proving their own integrity, showing fairness, and being willing to listen and serve others — while trusting others to do the same in return.

But cowards tend to trust no one, not even with the little things, which destroys any sense of trust. However, Courageous Police Leaders trust others, and do the little things that often build a tremendous sense of trust and understanding. For example, here's how a small-town Kansas police department achieved something that agencies in major cities with multi-million-dollar budgets rarely get right. And it's not about location, or size of the department—it's about trust, plain and simple.

The 10 Minute Rule

Sheriff Gareth Hoffman of the Dickinson County (Kansas) Sheriff's Department understands the community he serves. He was born and raised in the county. And he knows the people who live there as well as he knows the bumps on the backroads. But what Sheriff Hoffman knows best, is that the most important asset of his department is the trust of the community. And to keep that trust, his deputies must honor the "10 Minute Rule."

Here's how it works. When a deputy responds to a 911 call, they are expected to handle it and do whatever it takes to get the job done. But afterward, deputies are required to spend "10 minutes" more at the scene talking and listening to people in the community. It's during those 10 minutes that Hoffman says the real value of public service transpires. That's when deputies and the people involved can get to know each other and better understand each other—and learn to trust each other.

In contrast, cowardly leaders tend to treat people as objects: they're just a means to an end, and something you deal with going from call to call without any real concern. And the sooner you're done with one call, the sooner you can get to all those other calls that are holding.

This approach tends to fail miserably at developing any sense of trust with the community—and the kind of trust that helps prevent crime problems in the first place.

However, Courageous Police Leaders like Sheriff Hoffman get it right. They know that building and maintaining trust is critical. And they know that just a little adjustment in how they respond to calls for service can make a big difference. Speaking of, we've analyzed law enforcement agencies big and small, and Hoffman's "10 Minute Rule" has proven to be more powerful than hundreds of "community outreach" programs and "community partnership" initiatives.

The "10 Minute Rule" is brilliantly simple. And it does so much in building trust within the community and getting much-needed support in return. Yet it doesn't depend upon some fancy paradigm, or political initiative or "transformation." Instead, it puts an easy-to-follow rule in place and puts the responsibility and control for building trust in the hands of every single law enforcement officer—which builds trust all the way around.

4. COURAGEOUS POLICE LEADERS
RESPOND (INSTEAD OF REACT)

"Ponder and deliberate before you make a move..."
—*Sun Tzu*

Courageous Police Leaders understand the power of doing the right things at the right time. They understand when "strategic patience" makes sense, and when inaction does not. And by making a habit of thinking before acting, Courageous Police Leaders typically *respond* instead of *react*—and they rarely *over-react.*

They also excel at responding instead of reacting because unlike cowards, they typically don't let their egos, emotions, and external pressures influence their decisions or deeds. And instead of creating confusion and compromising the law enforcement profession, Courageous Police Leaders often deliberately respond by keeping what's best for their agencies, their communities, and the profession in mind.

This may sound a bit philosophical, but *responding*, instead of *reacting*, is critically important. Hundreds of careers have been cut short by emotional, knee-jerk reactions. And of course the media and the enemies of law enforcement are always ready to pounce and seize an opportunity whenever cowardly leaders overreact.

Fortunately, Courageous Police Leaders know this quite well. They know how to beat the enemy at their own game by responding instead of reacting. And there's probably nothing more frustrating for the enemy than trying to bait a coward to react, only to encounter a cool-headed Courageous Police

Leader who brushes off stress and confusion and offers deliberate responses—even in the middle of absolute chaos.

The difference between responding and reacting also has a lot to do with how Courageous Police Leaders actually lead. Since cowards typically think about themselves, they tend to overlook plenty of other key factors involved, which often leads them straight into the traps and tricky situations Courageous Police Leaders tend to avoid. Courageous Police Leaders also have better leadership and decision-making habits. They typically obtain information, get answers, and consider the variables—before making a decision or taking action. This doesn't mean they take forever; it just means they make the best use of whatever time they have to exercise due diligence.

Courageous Police Leaders are also the ones who take a few deep breaths to prevent themselves from reacting. They also tend to pause for a moment to step back and take a mental tally of the issues and challenges at hand—and to separate unrelated issues and incidents from clouding their judgment. Unlike cowards, Courageous Police Leaders let others respond first, which isn't only courteous, it's a smart way to keep their own emotions in check while gaining the benefit of hearing the opinions and advice of others.

Of course, these are just some of the ways that Courageous Police Leaders take emotion and knee-jerk reactions out of the equation. But perhaps overall, Courageous Police Leaders know that just because others are demanding a response, that doesn't mean a response is warranted or necessary, or that they must frantically respond to frantic demands.

For example, those who know Cambridge (Massachusetts) Police Commissioner Branville Bard Jr., would hardly be surprised to hear him described as being cool-headed under pressure, or as a man who typically challenges chaos with detailed, informative responses. Commissioner Bard is the real deal. And he leads by example in thoughtful ways, such as working Veteran's Day so that another officer who served in the military can have time off with his family.[3] Although perhaps Bard's response to a controversial video best exemplifies his clarity and his courage—and the ways that Courageous Police Leaders should respond to chaos.

In April 2018, Cambridge officers responded to a call of a naked man under the influence of drugs—yes, one of *those* calls. As officers struggled to arrest the combative subject, bystanders gathered on the sidewalks and in the street to confront officers and record the incident on their cellphones. Of course, videos of the incident prompted an outcry of police brutality not only among Harvard students in Cambridge, but across the nation.[4]

Yet it is in the midst of chaos that Courageous Police Leaders often shine. Cambridge Mayor Marc McGovern called the video "disturbing" and stated that "…Black Lives Matter, but it must be true in practice as well."[5] But instead of falling into the political traps, Commissioner Bard took a more

---

[3] Marc Levy, "Police Commissioner Bard Takes Day's Shift of Coast Guard Veteran to Observe Holiday," *Cambridge Day*, November 10, 2017.

[4] Katharine Seelye and Jess Bidgood, "Video Shows Police Tackling and Punching Black Harvard Student," *The New York Times*, April 16, 2018.

[5] John Hillard, "Videos Show Cambridge Officer Striking Black Harvard Student," *The Boston Globe*, April 15, 2018.

courageous approach: he stayed focused on policing and didn't *react* to all the chaos. Instead, Bard cut through all the nonsense, stayed focused on the facts—and *responded* by explaining how:

> "numerous attempts were made by the officers to calm down the male but they were met with opposition and hostility… That video also shows that the male wasn't compliant while he was on the ground… he was flailing, kicking…"[6]

And when asked about the officers involved in the presumed "brutality," Bard *responded* with a remarkable show of support for their actions—along with factual clarifications that are crucial for thwarting chaos:

> "I absolutely do support the officers. You have to judge their actions within the context of a rapidly, evolving situation..." and not within an ideal construct... we operate in a practical world."

Indeed, if the law enforcement profession had more courageous leaders like Bard—who respond so well when faced with controversy while showing support for officers—there'd be a lot less chaos and nonsense going around.

---

[6] Jonah Berger, "Police Commissioner Says He 'Absolutely' Supports Officers Who Arrested Harvard Student," *The Harvard Crimson,* April 16, 2018.

5. COURAGEOUS POLICE LEADERS CHALLENGE ASSUMPTIONS—AND ACCEPT ACCOUNTABILITY

"Ninety-nine percent of all failures come from people
who have a habit of making excuses." —*George Washington Carver*

Even if you just glance at the headlines now and again, it seems there's always some cowardly police leader confusing and conflating "assumptions" and "accountability." Fortunately, Courageous Police Leaders understand that although they're two different things, they're related, and they can cause plenty of chaos when they're mishandled.

Just for reference, an *assumption* is a claim that something is true. And whether they're based upon opinions or feelings, or deliberate lies and myths, assumptions often have little to do with facts and evidence these days. Separately, *accountability* occurs when someone is willing to be responsible—and held accountable—for their words and actions.

And here's how cowards get things mixed up. Cowards will often respond to assumptions as if they were true—no matter how ridiculous the assumptions may seem or sound. And they'll pretend to be "accountable"—only to find someone else to blame and hold responsible for just about any assumption or accusation people can make against law enforcement these days.

Courageous Police Leaders know better. They understand that people will say just about anything, to get away with just about anything. And facts be damned, an opinion or a feeling is all that's necessary to be "justified" in making an assumption or accusation these days. And it's pretty hard to ignore how some people expect whatever they assume will morph into "truth by popularity"—and bring them the instant gratification they deserve *according to their personal interests,* all within the time it takes to say something or share something on social media.[7] Even worse, it's as though they expect their assumptions—regardless of the actual facts—to have meaning and merit, and expect them to be influential.

Courageous Police Leaders can see through the assumptions—whether they're disguised as narratives, hashtags, t-shirt slogans, protest signs, or demands for an apology. But unlike cowardly leaders who run from controversy, Courageous Police Leaders don't ignore assumptions and accusations—they challenge them.

Indeed, the enemies of law enforcement have been quite successful in using assumptions and wild accusations to get cowardly leaders to respond. Of course, they're using assumptions and accusations like propaganda to confuse weak-minded leaders and get them to respond, or even worse "take action"—by pretending to be accountable for little more than an assumption or a lie.

However, when Courageous Police Leaders respond to assumptions with tact and professionalism—and take assumptions to task—it's as though the assumptions of social justice "warriors" and other enemies hit an impenetrable wall; they fall apart, if not disintegrate. And without a doubt, calling out an assumption, and the lack of merit behind it, can go a long way toward shutting down lies and myths before they create widespread chaos.

---

[7] Anthony Turner, "Generation Z: Technology and Social Interest," The Journal of Individual Psychology 71 (2, Summer 2015): 103-113.

Here's something else that Courageous Police Leaders get right. When assumptions or accusations are more than just lies and myths, and actually have merit and evidence to support them, Courageous Police Leaders accept accountability. Because unlike cowards who blame others, Courageous Police Leaders accept responsibility and hold themselves accountable, and they do so in the genuine sense—they're not pretending to be accountable only to pass the blame like cowards do.

Courageous Police Leaders also excel at shutting down assumptions, accusations, and propaganda. And they take on accountability in admirable, if not noble ways. But they also do something else when it comes to accountability: they practice it. That may sound a bit strange—after all, how does anyone practice accountability?

It's simple actually. Courageous Police Leaders give others permission to give them criticism and feedback about things they do well, and things they can do better. Which can help go a long way to breaking down the barriers to being responsible and accountable.

Basically, it works like this. A Courageous Police Leader will pick two, three, or more people—regardless of their rank—and give them permission to speak their minds, share their opinions, and criticize their behavior. This may seem unbearable at first, but after regularly speaking with their "accountability partners," many Courageous Police Leaders soon find themselves craving constructive criticism and feedback. That's because the routine feedback helps them improve, and become more adaptable, more responsible, and more aware.

It takes courage to open up and let others criticize you. But that's just it: Courageous Police Leaders know that it's a lot better to practice accountability and get feedback from people they can confide in and trust— instead of being forced to get better at handling accountability in far more embarrassing, if not career-ending ways.

It takes courage to open up and let others criticize you. So be courageous.

---

6. COURAGEOUS POLICE LEADERS ANTICIPATE CHAOS

> "Fight for the things that you care about, but do it in a way
> that will lead others to join you." —*Ruth Bader Ginsburg*

Courageous Police Leaders vigilantly scan for potential threats. They look for anything that can potentially cause personal and professional harm. And when you know your enemy, and you know their tricks and strategies, it's a whole lot easier to recognize the threats they pose. Courageous Police Leaders not only do an outstanding job at recognizing enemies and the threats they pose; they're masters at outsmarting them.

Outsmarting a potential threat doesn't mean going on the offensive and "striking first," although that may very well be necessary sometimes. It's more about being prepared for whatever the enemies of law enforcement may say or do in a particular situation—and being ready to respond and mitigate the chaos that may likely ensue. And when the unforeseeable happens, it involves staying focused on what matters most to law enforcement, even when there's nothing but critics, cowards, and chaos all around. Hopefully, the following example explains a bit more about how courageous leaders anticipate and outsmart the enemy.

Getting Ahead of "Getting Away with Murder"

On July 19, 2018 in Clearwater, Florida, a spat over a handicapped parking spot turned fatal. One man pushed another man to the ground—who then pulled a gun and fired the fatal shot that killed the man who pushed him.

This was not an officer-involved shooting and officers were not even there when the shooting occurred. Nonetheless, Pinellas County Sheriff Bob Gualtieri anticipated the chaos that would likely arise, especially since plenty of people were already outraged. Making matters worse, recent revisions to Florida's "stand your ground" law prevented the immediate arrest of the shooter, according to Sheriff Gualtieri.

After watching video of the incident, one could understand how the whole situation could have been avoided, and how the shooting could have been avoided as well. However, what's not so obvious are the procedural changes that came about in the latest revisions of Florida's "Stand Your Ground" law. Or put another way, it would be a bit much to expect that everyone who watched the video would understand that of course, the shooting was subject to Florida Statute 776.032, and therefore, the Pinellas County Sheriff's Department was precluded from making an arrest without further investigation. Instead, it was far more likely that most people who watched the video wondered why in the world the sheriff's department "refused" to arrest a cold-blooded killer, or something similar. Regardless of public opinion, the Pinellas County Sheriff's Department was not letting someone get away with murder, but following the "Stand Your Ground" law and its new procedures in textbook fashion.

Sheriff Gualtieri held a press conference to help explain the circumstances and quell the chaos. In his opening remarks, he made a very important distinction: "... I don't make the law; I enforce the law."[8]

---

[8] Evan Donovan, "Sheriff Explains Why "Stand Your Ground" Shooter Is Not Arrested," *WFLA.com,* July 22, 2018.

And to clarify the recent changes by the state legislature, Sheriff Gualtieri focused on the facts, and he read directly from Florida Statute 776.032(3):

> "A law enforcement agency may use standard procedures for investigating the use or threatened use of force as described in subsection (1), *but the agency may not arrest the person for using or threatening to use force* unless it determines that there is probable cause that the force that was used or threatened was unlawful."[9]

In a perfect world, someone from the state attorney's office would hold such a press conference. Or at least, they would at least step in to explain how the law applies to the circumstances of this unfortunate incident—and how the sheriff's department wasn't "letting a murderer walk free."

The shooting landed the Pinellas County Sheriff's Department in the middle of controversy and chaos. But instead of trying to avoid it all, Sheriff Gualtieri courageously took a proactive approach: he held a press conference, showed the video, and explained how the law applies to the circumstances of the incident. Gualtieri also faced the criticism head on, and expressed genuine concern and understanding:

> "I just ask everybody to understand—and there are a whole bunch of people, I know—and I've already got emails about it. People are already starting to voice concern about it, and I understand that. I don't make the law. But I'm going to enforce the law and I'll enforce it fairly as the legislature has directed that it be enforced."

---

[9] FLA. STAT. § 776.032(2) (2018); emphasis added.

But it didn't take long before national and international news media began touting headlines suggesting that the department let someone get away with murder.[10] Like many Courageous Police Leaders, Sheriff Gualtieri anticipated the chaos. He realized that his decision to follow the procedures in legislation was by no means an easy one, and by no means easy to understand. And he anticipated how others would likely criticize his decision. Plenty of politicians, police leaders, and activists took part in assaulting his decision. And plenty of criminal justice professionals also questioned Gualtieri's decision—even the NRA made its opposition known.[11]

However, Sheriff Gualtieri's handling of the situation certainly outsmarted his critics and his enemies. The shooter was arrested a few weeks later, as Gualtieri had intimated. He understood that arresting someone making a "Stand Your Ground" defense required following procedure, even though few seemed willing to make an effort to understand what the law or the procedure entailed.

And as far as outsmarting the enemy goes, since all the controversy erupted, Sheriff Gualtieri "has become a formidable force, one lawmakers bow to and activists seek out, knowing his opinion holds weight."[12]

---

[10] Robert Gearty, "Florida Sheriff Says "Stand Your Ground" Law Prevents Arrest in Fatal Shooting in Parking Spot Dispute," *FoxNews.com*, July 22, 2018.

[11] Patricia Mazzei, "N.R.A. Joins Questioning of Florida Sheriff in 'Stand Your Ground' Case," *The New York Times*, July 31, 2018.

[12] Kathryn Varn, "Pinellas Sheriff Bob Gualtieri is Now the Star Cop in Florida Politics. Who is He, and How Did He Get There?" *Tampa Bay Times*, May 9, 2019.

Of course, his rise in popularity didn't happen overnight, but his ability to anticipate chaos certainly had something to do with making him stand out. This is just one example of how anticipating chaos can be a smart move—and how being courageous can be contagious, particularly when you stick to the facts, follow the law, and do what's best for law enforcement.

Predicting chaos is like winning the battle before it even begins...

7. COURAGEOUS POLICE LEADERS LISTEN AND LEARN

> "Wise men talk because they have something to say;
> fools, because they have to say something." —*Plato*

It takes courage to admit you don't know everything. It's not a weakness by any means. It's actually a tremendous source of strength. And it helps explain something that sets Courageous Police Leaders apart from the rest: they listen and learn from others.

Unlike cowardly leaders who always seem to have something to say, Courageous Police Leaders are far more contemplative, if not silent. That's not because they're not paying attention—it's because they're listening and thinking. And without getting too deep into theory, they understand that listening is a skill, and a tremendously important one in the law enforcement profession.

For one thing, listening helps Courageous Police Leaders avoid embarrassment by saying the wrong thing, or speaking up at the wrong time. It also helps them better understand problems and develop better solutions. That's why Courageous Police Leaders tend to appreciate clarifications and key details—which cowards often regard as "pushback" or people just "overcomplicating things." And while cowards tend to be dismissive, or rely upon generalizations because they're too lazy to listen to the details, Courageous Police Leaders listen carefully. This allows them to think and learn, but also help control and focus discussions.[13]

Yes, by listening carefully, Courageous Police Leaders can tune into what others are saying—and what they're not saying—and the significance of it all. And by listening and paying attention, they often gain tremendous insight and can guide discussions accordingly. This is how the art and skill of listening allows Courageous Police Leaders to understand things that cowardly leaders often miss, or fail to understand.

While that may have a lot to do with what goes on inside the minds of Courageous Police Leaders, it also has a lot to do with their appearance and bearing on the outside. It's easy to spot the differences between leaders who listen and genuinely care—and those who could care less about anything anyone else has to say. Ultimately, it makes a big difference in trust. We tend to trust people who listen with patience and sincerity. And why should we trust someone who isn't even listening at all?

Listening is necessary to learn from mistakes
While it takes tremendous courage to listen to advice, perhaps it takes even more courage to listen to criticism, or discussions about one's own personal mistakes. But that's something else that sets Courageous Police Leaders apart from the rest. Not only do they listen, but they listen and learn from the mistakes of others, along with their own mistakes.

---

[13] Bernard Ferrari, *Power Listening: Mastering the Most Critical Business Skill of All* (New York: Penguin, 2012).

This isn't just self-help nonsense. It's essential for leading by example. And it's absolutely necessary to help others learn from mistakes, so they can avoid them as well. Listening and learning from mistakes is how real progress is made—and how embarrassing, if not deadly mistakes are often avoided.

For example, the New Orleans Police Department (NOPD) has its share of past mistakes and blemishes.[14] But instead of avoiding them, courageous NOPD leaders realized how the department had a tremendous opportunity to learn from its past mistakes and make real progress, and avoid repeating them again. In fact, they're making an EPIC effort to do so. As in EPIC, the acronym for Ethical Policing Is Courageous—the NOPD's innovative approach toward preventing police misconduct.

EPIC instructors understand the importance of recognizing and speaking up about mistakes in the making. They also understand that when officers learn to listen better, it becomes easier for them to "accept constructive criticism." Which goes a long way toward preventing misconduct from becoming necessary in the first place. Incidentally, one of the EPIC instructors, veteran NOPD officer Jacob Lundy, offered a bit of advice well worth remembering about listening and understanding. Lundy explained how "people can understand the mistakes... It's the cover-ups that cause so many problems."[15]

---

[14] Leonard Moore, *Black rage in New Orleans: Police brutality and African-American activism from World War II to Hurricane Katrina.* (Baton Rouge: Louisiana State University Press, 2010).

[15] Emily Lane, "In 'EPIC' Effort, New Orleans Police Work to Stop Officer Misconduct Before It Happens," *The Times-Picayune,* January 14, 2017.

At the core of the EPIC program is the idea that police misconduct and complaints can be averted when officers have the courage to "speak up" and intervene.[16] Which by the way, also depends upon having the courage to listen. And if there's any doubt that courage isn't contagious, dozens of other departments are taking part in the EPIC program, or have expressed interest in adopting it for their training in their departments.[17]

The EPIC program is just one example of how being courageous by listening and learning from mistakes can have a profound effect upon law enforcement efforts. And it's a great example of how Courageous Police Leaders understand that it's not just what they say that counts—but how they listen as well.

The key to guiding discussions and debates comes not from speaking to others, but from listening to them.

---

[16] Jonathan Aronie and Christy Lopez, "Keeping Each Other Safe: An Assessment of The Use of Peer Intervention Programs to Prevent Police Officer Mistakes and Misconduct, Using New Orleans' EPIC Program as A Potential National Model," *Police Quarterly* (September 2017): 295-321.

[17] Amy Novotney, "Preventing Police Misconduct," *American Psychological Association: Monitor on Psychology* 49, no. 9 (October 2017): 30.

A MISTAKE IN FORGETTING TO LISTEN

It would have been just another Tuesday morning. I was making my usual rounds gathering up information to share at the weekly staff meeting. But then the call came in—half a dozen people overdosed on K2 (a powerful synthetic cannabinoid known to alter the mind and cause wild and sometimes dangerous behavior). The drug, legally sold in head shops and some convenience stores, had recently taken the city by storm. Ten ambulances were dispatched to the first scene and within an hour we had 19 people in serious condition. By nightfall, 28 people were transported to area hospitals.

Panic also spread quickly throughout the city, and city leaders and the media were demanding answers. Personally, I was pissed off; I took great pride in the area that I commanded, and my team had worked particularly hard on keeping downtown safe—and these overdoses were about to ruin all of our hard work. And that's saying nothing about the tragedies and hardships these unfortunate overdoses could likely cause.

A few hours later, I gathered up the team and wanted to hear their solutions for putting a stop to this problem ASAP. I had my own solutions, but I wanted to hear what members of the team had to say—or so I thought.

One officer said we needed to seize every piece of K2 we found and test it for illegal drugs. That could be part of the solution, but it wasn't the solution. Another officer explained how we should go after the dealers. Again, that was clearly part of the solution, but not *the solution* either. Another officer pitched another idea, and then a few more did the same.

They were all good ideas, in part, but none of them offered the end-game solution. I told them I wanted something that would actually eradicate the problem, and fast.

Another officer was about to speak up, but in hindsight, it seems I had already shut down. Officer David Pyle was new to the unit. He was a quiet guy, but his skills and work ethic were unmatched. I was about to pack it in when David spoke up and boldly said, "we have to go after the source." Instead of listening, I began to press him, as though I had already dismissed whatever he had to say. David stood his ground and explained how while on patrol, he learned about a convenience store that was selling a lot of K2. David was also aware of a legal loop hole they were exploiting and how that allowed them to sell significant quantities of it.

In response, I gave a short and simple mandate: "Shut the store down by the 10 o'clock news." Within a few hours, a bunch of good cops ran a search warrant, seized a lot of K2, and ultimately shut the store down for good (it seems they could no longer sustain their business model selling candy bars and beer).

I was proud of the team. We made a huge impact preventing others from overdosing, and protecting the new spirit of the downtown area. But admittedly, this could have been a tremendous failure. Of course I knew the important leadership lesson about the importance of listening to others. It wasn't that I set out to ignore what David or anybody else had to say. And I didn't consciously make up my mind to be judgmental or dismissive. But at some point, after not hearing what I wanted to hear, I stopped listening—and I almost dismissed David's excellent idea, which led to quick-thinking, outstanding results, and plenty of high-fives.

Listening—truly listening—is a skill. I knew this, but at that point, I hadn't fully put it into practice. Or at least, I didn't have the skills or the stamina to hear what others had to say for very long while under pressure. Thankfully, it was a great leadership lesson for me, and a mistake that I most certainly learned from. Indeed, Courageous Police Leaders must listen—and always listen—because even after 99 bad ideas, the next one could be transformational.

—Travis Yates

8. COURAGEOUS POLICE LEADERS
HELP—AND SEEK HELP

"If you want to do a few small things right, do them yourself.
If you want to do great things and make a big impact,
learn to delegate." —*John Maxwell*

Being a Courageous Police Leader isn't a solo mission. In fact, many would say it's quite the opposite. For one thing, courageous leadership involves being able to lead—and lead well with other leaders. It also involves being able to delegate and share responsibility with others, including sharing leadership responsibilities. And it involves knowing when and how to help others, and when to ask others for help.

With that in mind, Courageous Police Leaders understand that helping isn't just something you do—it's something you must understand. Meanwhile, cowardly police leaders tend to get this all wrong. Cowards are often unable to effectively delegate to their subordinates because they're either power-hungry control freaks, or have burned so many bridges that all they can do is make demands, micro-manage, and command others to help. And they tend to avoid asking their superiors or peers for help and guidance out of fear of seeming weak or incompetent.

Cutting through all the nonsense, Courageous Police Leaders understand that helping others and seeking help has a lot to do with honesty. If you're honest with yourself and know your limitations, you'll know when you need help and how to ask for it. And when it comes to helping others, Courageous Police Leaders often do so proactively, without being asked, or in ways that are most comfortable and most helpful for others. And when it comes to leading with others, it isn't about being blindly obedient, or letting personal ambitions get in the way. Granted, this may seem like making a big deal out of nothing. But knowing how to help, how to ask for help, and how to help others lead can sometimes make or break a career.

For example, Bill Bratton, the former top cop at NYPD, LAPD, and the Boston PD, admitted that his biggest mistake in serving under New York Mayor Rudy Giuliani was this: "I didn't stay in his headlights."[18] In other words, Bratton didn't stay close enough to Giuliani and his leadership vision, and he wasn't helping Giuliani lead. However, like many Courageous Police Leaders, Bratton learned from his mistakes:

> "I worked very hard working for the next three mayors I worked for, to stay within their headlights... Leadership, sometimes, is the idea that you're the lone wolf, if you will, but oftentimes leadership is also learning to stay within the parameters of those that you are working for—other leaders."

Bratton mentions the idea of being "a lone wolf," which highlights a rather interesting paradox in the law enforcement profession. We're supposed to be fearlessly brave and willing to run down dark alleys to face all kinds of dangers. But at the same time, we entrust our lives to our backers, dispatchers, and others to keep us safe and help us get the job done. Yet while so much of law enforcement is a team effort, it's should seem really strange that asking for help remains stigmatized. And asking for help from

---

[18] Zack Guzman, "Bill Bratton Reveals What His "Biggest Mistake" Taught Him About Ambition," *CNBC.com,* July 13, 2018.

other officers or superiors—or even the community—can definitely cause some officers to feel judged, if not ostracized whenever cowards are around.[19] Consequently, some officers shy away from asking for help at the very times when they need it most.

Fortunately, the efforts of Courageous Police Leaders have started to change the misperceptions about helping others and asking for help. Unlike cowards, courageous leaders help others when needed and ask for help needed just the same, without getting caught up in feeling obligated or anxious to reciprocate. More importantly, Courageous Police Leaders are typically pro-active when it comes to helping others, and they're often already pitching in before anyone has to ask them for help. Yet they do so without barging in, or taking over, or making others feel incompetent, as cowards often do.

Yet perhaps most importantly, Courageous Police Leaders are promoting a culture of mutual support—beyond words, and beyond empty, feel-good promises. They understand the irony that while law enforcement officers are supposed to help kids and kittens, and everyone and everything in between, we are reluctant to help each other in a genuine sense without second-guessing ourselves or wondering what others might think, or letting ambitions get in the way. Of course, if an officer is involved in a shoot-out or a bad wreck, the cavalry will be there. Although if an officer needs help

---

[19] Alysa Lambert and Camela Steinke, "Negative Perceptions of Asking for Support in Law Enforcement: Potential Benefit Avoidance," *International Journal of Police Science & Management* 17 (June 1, 2015).

learning how to use new equipment, or understanding a new procedure, or working on leadership skills, it may seem like the world disappeared.

It is in these moments that Courageous Police Leaders tend to stand out. They're typically the ones who break the ice when others obviously need help. And without being sarcastic, Courageous Police Leaders typically ask for clarification, to better understand the vision, strategy, and goals that other leaders have in mind. They're also the ones who anticipate, and spot the "roadblocks" and the "pitfalls" so their subordinates get the help they need without any embarrassment, and often without anyone even realizing it. And unlike cowardly leaders, Courageous Police Leaders certainly don't put people down when they ask for help. Instead, they often encourage if not reward those who seek help and support from others.

Courageous Police Leaders also understand how "letting others help others," is an excellent way to share responsibility and get things done more efficiently and effectively. For example, when a new crime problem pops up, Courageous Police Leaders may not rush to offer an immediate solution. Instead, they'll seek help from others. This accomplishes at least three things. First, it lets others become more aware of the problem, and become more engaged in for working toward a solution. Second, it allows everyone involved to take advantage of the ideas, approaches, and tactics others have and combine them or improve upon them. And third, it inspires other leaders so they too become familiar with helping others and asking for help.

Indeed, Courageous Police Leaders know that "teachable moments" don't just happen *after* mistakes are made. They understand how some of the most important lessons can be learned *before* mistakes are made.

Help from A Disappearing Chief

Cowardly leaders tend to avoid the little things. And they practically avoid helping others with little things, yet want to be part of the big things so they can put their name on it or take credit for it. Courageous Police Leaders do the opposite. And they understand how helping others with the "small stuff" can make a big impact.

I was shocked one day when the Chief's aide called me. I was a rookie and my first thought was that I did something wrong. However, the truth wasn't much better. Every month, Chief Ron Palmer rode with a patrol officer, and the Chief's aide called to let me know that I was next on the list. I wasn't exactly thrilled, and I didn't exactly count myself as being lucky having to take the time to wash the car, polish the brass, and then work a shift with my new "partner," who I imagined would be watching every single move I made. I didn't feel like I did something wrong, but couldn't help thinking that I was about to do something wrong, if not everything wrong.

That night, the chief showed up, and after he introduced himself, we were in the car heading to our first call. Fortunately, it was just a "routine" report call. I figured there was little chance for me to screw it up, and figured not much could go wrong here.

But of course, things certainly went wrong. As I was interviewing the caller about the burglary and reviewing my notes, I noticed the chief disappeared. He was gone—nowhere to be found. He wasn't even with me for an hour and I already lost him—or he was so appalled I thought, that he just left to begin the proceedings to fire me.

I was about to give up and give up all hope, when I saw the chief walking to me out of the darkness. I was expecting a reprimand of some sort, or at least some advice about what I was doing wrong. Instead, Chief Palmer came back with a notepad with the names, addresses, and contact information of the neighbors in the area—yes, the chief of police canvassed the neighborhood for me. Apparently, an explanation was necessary to overcome the shock on my face, and Chief Palmer explained, "I canvassed the area for you. I thought it would help with your investigation."

I was floored, flabbergasted—you name it. To think the Chief of Police just helped me, a rookie, conduct a canvass was unheard of, at least to me. My apprehensions became awe, as I could hardly believe that a chief would help a rookie like that, and it left me wondering the rest of the night. Admittedly, it was a long shift, but as Chief Palmer walked away that night, he stopped and said "Travis, you are a good cop. Great job tonight."

I was standing beside myself. Not only did the Chief know my name, he helped me with a routine chore, and then offered me encouragement. Needless to say, the chief's words and actions left quite an impression upon my rookie-self back then.

But as time went on, and I gained experience and promotions, I grew to resent what the chief did for me that night. I thought if the chief could help a rookie and offer encouragement, why couldn't every leader of every other rank do that? I sort of expected it, but after encountering and enduring too many forms of cowardly leadership, I soon became disappointed, which grew to a resentment of sorts. The chief set a perfect example I thought, yet it seemed many other leaders and supervisors failed to follow his lead—or failed to just help out for the sake of lending a hand.

At some point, I realized just how special—and how necessary—it was that the chief offered to help, and offered encouragement as well. If you don't think this is a big deal, think for a minute about how many other leaders and supervisors would show up on a call, and help out with the little things? Of course the cowards won't. But thankfully there are a growing number of Courageous Police Leaders out there who understand that a "huge success" is often built on "small details" and how helping out with the little things can make a big difference.

—Travis Yates

9. COURAGEOUS POLICE LEADERS LEAD BY EXAMPLE

"It is better to have less thunder in the mouth,
and more lightning in the hand" — *Apache proverb*

Although cowards can "talk the talk," it takes courage to "walk the walk" and truly lead by example. As with most things cowardly leaders *think* they're doing, they're rarely leading by example. Well, except for being an example of *what not to do* when it comes to police leadership. Leading by example takes courage and commitment, and it's something that Courageous Police Leaders practice often.

For example, during his swearing-in ceremony, Birmingham (Alabama) Police Chief Patrick Smith made his intentions about leading by example quite clear:

> "Taking over as Birmingham chief of police is not something I take lightly. This requires full-scale leadership, something I've always strived to exemplify, as a marine, as an officer and as a person."[20]

Chief Smith's remarks may seem like the kind of thing you'd expect someone to say after taking a victory lap, or becoming the top cop. Yet while he may be speaking about himself, he's also doing something that many Courageous Police Leaders do: he's signaling the commitment to "full-scale" leadership that he strives to "exemplify," along with the conduct he expects from others.

---

[20] Carol Robinson, "'It's a New Day': Birmingham Police Chief, Top Brass Sworn in to Office," *AL.com,* July 27, 2018.

Precisely *how* that is accomplished is a whole other matter (if not an entire book). There's a lot to be said about different leadership styles and the pros and cons of each. But perhaps one of the leading advantages of "leading by example" is that it provides a practical model that others can readily observe and imitate.[21] It's also a demonstration of conduct that others can observe and constructively criticize—which courageous leaders allow others to do.

Indeed, by choosing to lead by example, Courageous Police Leaders hold themselves out to be role models. And if that alone doesn't take plenty of courage, they do so knowingly, and fully aware that their subordinates and fellow leaders will either "follow" and perhaps imitate them—or despise them for failing to live up to their own expectations, much like cowardly hypocrites. Choosing to lead by example will influence the conduct and behavior of others—one way or another—for sure.[22]

Along with influencing conduct and behavior, leading by example also influences attitude, which is one of the most important, yet most often overlooked aspects of police leadership. Although it's emerging in police leadership training, adopting a courageous leader's attitude still isn't something that officers deliberately or even consciously decide to do. Few people actually say, "I'm going to use their attitude."

---

[21] Richard R. Johnson, "Leading by Example: Supervisor Modeling and Officer-Initiated Activities," *Police Quarterly* 18, (3, September 2015): 223-243.

[22] Robin Engel, "How Police Supervisory Styles Influence Patrol Officer Behavior," in *Critical Issues in Policing: Contemporary Readings,* Roger Dunham and Geoffrey Alpert, eds., (Long Grove, Illinois: Waveland Press, 2015: 219-228.

Also, attitude isn't just something to "adjust." Although, when Courageous Police Leaders continually work on improving their approach to making decisions, how they handle situations, and interact with others, their attitude can bear tremendous influence upon others—and it can certainly make a significant difference.

For example, in 2016, when Sergeant Suzanna Dawson became the first supervisor in the 209-year history of the Granville (Ohio) Police Department, she noted the influence that her law enforcement family had upon her. And she also spoke about some of the key things she learned about leadership: "There's a new emphasis being placed on behavior and not just procedure. There's also more focus on attitudes than ever before."[23]

Sergeant Dawson not only spoke about the direction of leadership at the time, she also spoke to one of the key things about Courageous Police Leadership and leading by example: it involves not just what you do or what you say, but your "attitude"—how you think and act, and carry yourself.

Indeed it takes courage to lead by example, and subject one's self to the demands of "full-scale leadership," as Chief Smith remarked. Yet that's exactly what Courageous Police Leaders do when they lead by example: they hold themselves fully accountable for practically everything they do or say, how they act, their attitude—basically everything about who they are becomes an example and subject to scrutiny.

---

[23] Craig McDonald, "Granville P.D. Has 1st Female Supervisor," *Newark Advocate,* July 6, 2016.

This may seem challenging, if not daunting. But it's also quite funny. That is, if you consider how cowardly leaders fail to realize how they lead by example as well, and are subject to scrutiny just the same—if not more because they're typically surrounded by chaos. However, unlike cowards, Courageous Police Leaders tend to not make fools of themselves; instead they realize and acknowledge how no matter what, they're leading by example—and that it's best to make a commitment and a deliberate effort to strive and set the best example (and not the worst). Besides, putting in the effort to lead by example can be transformative, and not only for the people "following" by example, but for courageous leaders themselves.

For example, Sergeant Dawson not only became the first female supervisor of her department, she continued to rise through the ranks. And after 28 years of service, she "retired" as a lieutenant, only to become the first female Sergeant at Arms for the Ohio Senate. That's quite a long way from her first role in law enforcement as a dispatcher. And when Courageous Police Leaders lead by example, others take notice. In honoring Lieutenant Dawson's dedication and service, Granville Mayor Melissa Hartfield remarked, how Dawson did her job with "dedication and distinction, *leading by example* and earning the deep respect and gratitude of the citizens, Village Council, staff and her fellow officers." [24]

---

[24] Craig McDonald, "Lt. Dawson Retiring from Granville Police for Ohio Senate," *Newark Advocate*, July 6, 2016; emphasis added.

The law enforcement profession needs more leaders like Sergeant at Arms Dawson—leaders who have the courage to lead by example. Her dedication, her attitude, and her leadership approach, and accomplishments should be commended. But her efforts to lead by example, and those of many other Courageous Police Leaders like her, shouldn't just be commended, or imitated—they should become the norm.

10. COURAGEOUS POLICE LEADERS
STAY IN THE FIGHT

"If you are going through hell, keep going"
—*Winston Churchill*

The law enforcement profession can be unpredictable, to say the least. And sometimes we may find ourselves in the worst of situations—like when the only thing left to do is hope that your backers are charging hard and bringing hell with them to save you. Unfortunately, there are plenty of other situations where it takes a lot of courage to stay in the fight.

As a profession, we do pretty well at preparing for the worst in terms of physical confrontations. We understand the importance of training to handle situations with active shooters, barricaded subjects, armed robbery suspects, and the like. And overall, we're pretty good at training for the worst, hoping for the best, and staying in the fight. And some of us never give up.

But for some reason, we're hardly prepared for other kinds of confrontations. That is, while many of us would sacrifice our lives to save others, too many of us give up and give in all too easily when combating cowardly police leaders, social justice "warriors" and other enemies of law enforcement. As strange as it sounds, we think nothing of taking on the most violent criminals in dark alleys. Yet challenging the words of a coward behind a desk seems daunting somehow.

Some of us would rather get beat out of our uniforms than deal with bureaucracy or the pettiness of cowardly police leaders. And then there are others who prefer to complain about practically everything, and do nothing but complain. Needless to say, neither of these approaches are going to help win the fight—and neither help the Courageous Police Leaders who are fighting the good fight for us.

Courageous Police Leaders don't ignore cowardly leaders and other enemies of law enforcement. And they don't mistakenly believe that problems with and chaos, myths, and lies will go away by themselves. And they certainly aren't kidding themselves in believing that someone else is going to take care of things for them. Courageous Police Leaders know better. They know that there's nothing to be ashamed about when cowardly thugs ambush you in the dark of the night. And they also know there's absolutely no dignity whatsoever in letting cowardly leaders and our other enemies get the best of us, time and time again.

Granted, there will be plenty of times when circumstances may prevent us from taking a stand. However, Courageous Police Leaders pick their battles and their strategies wisely—because that's what it takes to stay in fight. They understand that there's no sense battling cowards and chaos if you're not going to gain an advantage to ultimately win the war. And much like the wisdom in Sun Tzu's *Art of War*, they know that sometimes it's better to forego a battle to win the war. Courageous Police Leaders know that it takes a special kind of courage and resistance to stay committed, and stay in the fight, especially when it seems like your "not speaking up" or just "doing nothing" at all.

The road to victory is hardly ever a direct one. And sometimes, the best strategies require plenty of patience, especially when it comes to avoiding the pitfalls, staying out of traps, and being wary of sabotage, which often require considerable time and effort. And yes, given the circumstances, sometimes the best thing to do is to avoid direct combat—but nonetheless seize the opportunity to observe and better understand the enemy. Likewise, when things seem to be headed "way off course," or "taking too long" and "getting nowhere," it takes tremendous courage to stay in the fight.

Overall, Courageous Police Leaders engage in smarter combat. While others are running around in a panic, or feeling anxious as though they *must* react, or have to respond, Courageous Police Leaders are calculating their next move. They know from experience that it takes time to understand the enemy and how to outsmart them. And after years of practice, some know intuitively just how to "respond."

Courageous Police Leaders also know that staying in the fight requires a dynamic range of effort. Sometimes just challenging a cowardly assumption, or asking a tough question is enough to send cowards running. And the cool-headedness and rationality of Courageous Police Leaders often leaves the enemy stammering at a loss for words when they're pressed for facts to explain their ridiculous opinions or directives. Other times, Courageous Police Leaders will use the enemy's own tactics against them, and get *them* to over-react or "lose it," or at least divide their focus and attention. Which tends to happen whenever the presumed (self-)righteousness of cowards and myth-makers is challenged by facts and clear-thinking. At the same time, whether it's evading, engaging, or completely surrounding the enemy to win the battle—if not the war—Courageous Police Leaders don't stop until they achieve what's best for the law enforcement profession. They don't give up, and they don't give in—they always stay in the fight.

PART III

BE

COURAGEOUS

FEAR NO BATTLE

"In the midst of chaos, there is also opportunity"
—Sun Tzu

There's no telling what the cowards, the chaos, and the circumstances have in store for the law enforcement profession in the future. As a Courageous Police Leader, you'll face many battles. But that's nothing to worry about. As Sun Tzu's wisdom reminds us, "if you know the enemy and know yourself, you need not fear the outcome of a hundred battles."

However, there's another aspect of Sun Tzu's ancient wisdom worth remembering even when you're outnumbered by cowards and surrounded by chaos, there's always an opportunity to gain an advantage and overcome your opponents. Absolutely, Courageous Police Leadership takes more than being courageous and not being a coward. It takes knowing *how to survive* and *how to combat* the cowards and the chaos. Granted, being a Courageous Police Leader demands courage—just as much as it involves art and skill, and plenty of strategy. What follows are some of the battles and challenges that Courageous Police Leaders have faced in the past, and will likely face again, along with some proven advice to help Courageous Police Leaders survive and win—and ultimately help the law enforcement profession make real progress.

BE LOYAL TO POLICING—NOT POLITICS

"Those who have one foot in the canoe, and one foot on the shore, are going to fall into the river" — *Tuscarora proverb*

Everything seems political these days. And it doesn't seem that America's preoccupation with politics is going to fade away anytime soon. So until America has had enough of "political correctness" and political nonsense, perhaps the most important thing a Courageous Police Leaders can do "politically" is to stay focused on policing—not politics.

This may sound strange if not counterintuitive, but it's absolutely necessary. Consider this simple fact: if Courageous Police Leaders do not stay focused on policing, who will? The cowardly leaders, the "look-at-me" politicians, and selfie-obsessed social justice "warriors," certainly aren't going to, that's for sure. And if for no other reason, Courageous Police Leaders must stay focused and advocate what's right for the law enforcement profession— because nobody else will.

But there's another reason as well. And that is, there is tremendous power in staying focused. If you pick up any business book written in the past 20 years, you'll likely find advice about how businesses should "focus on their core competencies" or how they should stay focused on "doing what they do best" to succeed. And if staying focused makes sense for business, it also makes sense for the "business" of law enforcement.

Staying focused on policing instead of politics is also a way to shut down many enemies of law enforcement before they even get started. This can be extremely advantageous since enemies often try to get police leaders to stray from crime-fighting and get involved in politics—so they can manipulate them and fold them into whatever anti-police agendas they're trying to promote. Yet perhaps the biggest advantage to staying focused is that it helps ensure that leadership decisions link directly to what's best for policing and the community—not political nonsense.

Granted, law enforcement means many things to many people, and just about everything to do with police work is being criticized and politicized nowadays. But in staying focused, Courageous Police Leaders can gain an advantage by emphasizing perhaps the most important—yet most overlooked—aspect of law enforcement: it's about *enforcing the law*. It's not about making the law, or debating how laws should be reformed, or what the consequences of breaking the law ought to be.

With all the political chaos swirling around these days, Courageous Police Leaders need to be the cool-headed, voices of reason who remind others that the purpose of law enforcement is to ensure public safety and fight crime; and that everything else is beyond the focus of law enforcement. To spell it out clearly: politics and policing are two different things.

Courageous Police Leaders understand the distinction, and they avoid all the political nonsense, and combat it whenever necessary. But cowardly police leaders, thanks to their inflated egos, try to do both and fail; they think they're doing what's best politically, and maybe what's best for law enforcement—but most of the time, all they're doing is failing miserably and leaving the law enforcement profession and the communities they serve to suffer the consequences amid confusion and chaos.

Having said all that, of course politics and policing overlap, and it would be naïve to think that they don't. Especially since the higher up the chain of command you go, the greater the political pressure and criticism. And so long as police chiefs are appointed by mayors or government officials, and sheriffs are elected by voters, policing will involve politics to some extent. That's not a problem in itself. But the significant problems show up whenever cowardly police leaders pay more attention to politics, and pay less attention to doing what's best for policing and public safety. Sometimes the consequences may amount to little more than "small town" political drama. But they can also lead to a political catastrophe—and sweeping reforms that can affect law enforcement agencies nationwide.

Staying focused can help prevent all the political "drama," but can also help thwart attempts at unfounded "reforms." Granted, this may demand truly courageous efforts. And sometimes doing what's best for policing and protecting communities may cost courageous leaders their jobs. But if Courageous Police Leaders are willing to sacrifice their lives in the line of duty, they should be willing to sacrifice their paychecks—otherwise, they're in the wrong profession, doing the wrong thing, for the wrong reasons.

But this isn't the real issue at hand, particularly since most of the political problems can be traced to cowardly leaders. They're the ones saying yes to everything that's politically popular, and promising everything to everybody. They're also the ones who allow every *(unsubstantiated)* accusation to become an internal investigation. And cowardly leadership is often the reason why even just the accusation of misconduct is all that's necessary to rewrite policy, or dole out unfair discipline.

Generally speaking, cowards can't seem to resist being political, and they often make political promises that compromise the law enforcement profession. Although they hardly seem to mind—especially since political busy-work makes them seem far more important. But what the cowards often forget is that the *appearance* of police work and *actual* police work are entirely different things. Incidentally, the difference is one of "Peel's Principles of Law Enforcement," which states:

> "The test of police efficiency is the *absence* of crime and disorder, not the *visible evidence* of police action dealing with them."[1]

Obviously, cowardly leaders are confused. And whenever they pay far too much attention to politics, they tend to get anxious about "looking busy." But the "absence of crime" is the true measure of police work, not the "visible evidence" of police work—which for cowards, amounts to little more than political busy-work in disguise.

---

[1] Thomas Svogun, *The Jurisprudence of Police: Toward a General Unified Theory of Law* (New York: Palgrave Macmillan, 2013), 89.

To put it another way, and perhaps more truthfully, whenever cowards *appear* to be doing something, they're often just being political—and probably doing more to *enable crime* instead of putting a stop to it. Political agendas rarely result in effective, long-term crime reduction. And that's because whenever politicians and cowardly police leaders fail to stay focused on law enforcement efforts, they often create more opportunities for criminals, and make it easier for them to get away with more and more. It's not hard to figure out: the less you do for cops; the more you do for criminals. And while (unnecessary) police "reforms" may seem politically popular, they often do nothing to help prevent crime—or deter crime—and criminals across America couldn't be happier.

BE RESPONSIBLE FOR POLICING (NOT IRRESPONSIBLY POLITICAL)

Without a doubt, in many communities throughout the country, crime problems have less to do with policing, and a whole lot more to do with politics. Unfortunately, far too many cities and towns have become playgrounds for political agendas, or "bouncy houses" for social advocacy. Instead of allowing law enforcement to stay focused on policing, many political "leaders" become blindly obsessed with political agendas and ambitions—and forsake their service to the public and public safety. The trick is to find opportunities to stand up and put a stop to this nonsense. And whenever politicians try to blame law enforcement for their own failed policies or political agendas, Courageous Police Leaders must seize every advantage and every opportunity to shut them down.

Fortunately, there are Courageous Police Leaders who are out there doing just that. They're standing up to the political nonsense, and the politicians themselves. Here's an example of what staying focused and combating political chaos looks like. It comes from Daryl Turner, the president of the Portland Police Association and a former Portland police officer, who wrote a letter to the mayor. Turner masterfully shifted the focus from politics— back to policing and public safety. He also mentions plenty of *visible evidence* of failed political policies, which is partly why his response is worth quoting entirely:

> *Our City has become a cesspool. Livability that once made Portland a unique and vibrant city is now replaced with human feces in businesses doorways, in our parks, and on our streets. Aggressive panhandlers block the sidewalks, storefronts, and landmarks like Pioneer Square, discouraging people from enjoying our City. Garbage-filled RVs and vehicles are strewn throughout our neighborhoods. Used needles, drug paraphernalia, and trash are common sights lining the streets and sidewalks of the downtown core area, under our bridges, and freeway overpasses. That's not what our families, business owners, and tourists deserve.*
>
> *Mayor Wheeler's public policies have failed. Record tax revenues are being brought into the City; yet what do we have to show for it? I am incensed that once again the Mayor has thrown Portland Police Officers under the bus instead of saying what we all know to be true: that his proposed solutions to our homelessness crisis have failed. What we need is for our City and County leaders to take responsibility for this crisis getting out of hand. They need to put forth actual solutions with actual results and stop throwing hard-earned taxpayer dollars down a black hole.*

True to form, instead of standing up and leading, Mayor Wheeler has reverted to the, "Is there some sort of profiling or implicit bias by the cops" rhetoric to smokescreen his own failed policies. Will investigating our officers result in more housing for the homeless? Will it provide more mental health or addiction resources for those in need? Will it resolve the livability issues that Portland residents and business owners face daily? Of course not! It's more of the same from the Mayor; failed policies and blaming others for his failures.

The Portland Police Bureau has not been given nearly enough resources to fulfill its small piece in addressing the homelessness crisis. We are understaffed. Officers are unable to spend the time needed to connect our homeless to necessary services, whether it be housing, mental health services, drug rehabilitation, or other resources. It's a recipe for failure to put the burden of the homelessness solution on the Police Bureau's shoulders and then give us insufficient resources to do the work.

The rank and file of the Portland Police Bureau are working tirelessly to improve livability in our City, preserve public safety, and connect our vulnerable communities to social services. We are the first line resource on the streets serving the public—including the homeless—every day with care and professionalism. The fact that our officers have become the scapegoats for Mayor Wheeler's failed public policies aimed at solving our homelessness crisis is insulting.

Portland Police Officers deserve better. Our families and communities deserve better. Our businesses deserve better. Our City deserves better!

Obviously, Turner is fed up with cowardly leadership and politics. Yet he stays focused on the expectations of the public and what's necessary to improve public safety. And while he points out the mayor's attempt to scapegoat the police department, Turner speaks up for police officers and the community—and addresses the evidence of the real problems at hand.

Granted, responding to criticism, adjusting to the political climate, and making *necessary* reforms are all part of effective law enforcement. But they should never be the sole focus of law enforcement leadership, and never the top priority. If the focus of law enforcement is public safety and fighting crime, then Courageous Police Leaders must stay focused on law enforcement. Indeed, the best thing Courageous Police Leaders can do politically is to stay focused on what's best for law enforcement and public safety.

Courageous Police Leaders must be gatekeepers: they must allow constructive criticism and necessary change—but keep political chaos out.

FOCUS ON DATA—NOT DELUSIONS

"Facts are stubborn things, but statistics are more pliable"
—*Mark Twain*

Statistics are often the basis of many accusations against law enforcement. And it seems social justice "warriors" and their allies love manipulating numbers to fabricate all kinds of myths. And the news media seem just as obsessed with using data and statistics to make all kinds of magical revelations about law enforcement activities. If it weren't for the reactions of cowardly police leaders, their efforts would be nothing but comedy. Instead of refuting their delusional claims, however, cowardly leaders are "taking action." And the chaos they create is unfortunately no laughing matter. That's why Courageous Police Leaders must know the enemies of law enforcement—and know how they manipulate statistics to fabricate lies and myths.

Whenever data and statistics get twisted around to criticize law enforcement, Courageous Police Leaders must stay focused. And that requires staying focused on two important aspects, at the least. First, when *credible* data and statistics point to real problems with law enforcement efforts, Courageous Police Leaders must face the numbers and the facts, and take accountability and action to fix them. Secondly, when the enemies of law enforcement try to manipulate statistics for the sake of myths and unfounded accusations, Courageous Police Leaders must counter such attempts—if not attack and destroy them—with careful forethought and counter-analysis, of course.

However, this presumes that the stats matter more than the motivations behind the stat-based accusations. But this isn't always the case, especially since statistics can be used to fabricate just about any lie. So whenever stats are tossed around as "evidence" to support whatever law enforcement can be blamed for, it's important to ask what's the intention of these so-called statistical "facts"—and what purpose are they supposed to serve?

Surprisingly, cowardly police leaders tend to forget to question statistics or their purpose. And consequently, plenty of battles have been lost by jumping into the numbers and overlooking the purpose and motivations behind the statistics. Details count, but Courageous Police Leaders cannot lose sight of the "bigger picture"—or the overall argument, and the overall context for the accusations.

To overcome this problem, it may help to approach it like any other tactical drill: when you see a stat, ask "what's this supposed to prove?"—and do it constantly until it becomes second nature. If the stats are reliable and the argument is valid, then there's reason to dive into the numbers. If the stats are questionable, or the purpose of them doesn't seem to make sense, then taking the stats to task may be counterproductive. And more often than not, many of the so-called "problems" stemming from data and statistics have little to do with actual law enforcement, and more to do with reckless accusations and *about* law enforcement.

THE DELUSION OF "DEMOGRAPHIC PARITY"

Data and statistics are used to support all kinds of faulty arguments and accusations against law enforcement. Although, perhaps the most common—and the most absurd—use of statistics involves the myth of "demographic parity": the idea that X% of a particular demography should magically correlate to the same X% of crimes, arrests, or whatever else. "Demographic parity" sounds ethical, but it's absurd and improbable, if not impossible.

Nevertheless, "demographic parity" often serves as a battle cry for social justice "warriors" and their attorney allies. Yet the most absurd thing about "demographic parity" is that cowardly leaders rarely challenge the idea or the so-called statistics used to support it, despite the nonsense and statistical improbability of it all.

Subsequently, "demographic parity" statistics have been used against law enforcement for quite some time. And all the "reforms" that have been implemented due to the disparities in "demographic parity" statistics have been catastrophic—if not demoralizing. Yet the worst of it is that countless accusations of alleged racial discrimination have been "proven" with little more than a few "statistics"—and the absolutely ridiculous assumption that law enforcement efforts *must* reflect "demographic parity." However, as attorney, political commentator, and author Heather Mac Donald emphasizes, "When we're talking about police activity, the relevant benchmark is crime, not population."[2]

---

[2] Eric Black, "Assessing Heather Mac Donald's Counter-Narrative About Blacks and Police," *MinnPost.com,* December 12, 2016.

Absolutely, the relevant benchmark for the effectiveness of law enforcement involves *crime*, not population—and certainly not the myth of "demographic parity." That's why Courageous Police Leaders must be diligent and shut down any attempt to manipulate statistics and decry a so-called lack of "demographic parity." Otherwise, statistics will continue to be manipulated and used against the law enforcement profession for all kinds of unsubstantiated accusations and so-called "reforms"—or perhaps "foundations for lucrative lawsuits" is a more accurate description.

For example, one of the most ridiculous attempts to use "demographic parity" statistics to "prove" how a law enforcement agency was racist occurred right after The Violent Crime Control and Law Enforcement Act was passed in 1994. The DOJ opened an investigation of the New Jersey State Police, which was accused of racial discrimination based upon the data and findings of one particular research statistician.[3] The researcher suggested "that cars with black occupants" accounted for about 15 percent of all traffic law violators. And according to the myth of "demographic parity," the New Jersey State Police *should have* only stopped 15 percent of cars with a black occupant. However, they stopped more than twice as many—35 percent of the cars that the New Jersey State Police stopped had a black occupant, either the driver or a passenger. Clearly the enormous demographic "disparity" between 15 percent and 35 percent could only be explained by racial discrimination.

---

[3] Stephen Rushin, "Federal Enforcement of Police Reform," *Fordham Law Review* 82 (2014): 3222.

Since the statistics obviously indicated a lack of "demographic parity"—as the researcher and police critics assumed—a more thorough investigation was launched. Subsequently, The Public Service Research Institute conducted a more comprehensive study of speeders along the New Jersey Turnpike using high-speed cameras linked to radar guns.

The study was supposed to provide statistics to validate how the New Jersey State Police discriminated against "black" and "Hispanic" drivers. After all, that's what the initial statistics *clearly indicated* according to the myth of "demographic parity," or in this case, the myth of "driving while black." [4] However, the data and statistics from the second study told a much different story. And much to the chagrin of politicians, attorneys, and police reformers, the results disproved the claims of racial discrimination practices. As reported in The New York Times in March 2002:

> "Those results startled officials in the state attorney general's office, who had assumed that the radar study would bolster their case that profiling was widespread. Instead, the study concluded that blacks make up 16 percent of the drivers on the turnpike and 25 percent of the speeders in the 65 m.p.h. zones, where complaints of profiling have been most common." [5]

---

[4] John Lamberth, "Driving While Black: A Statistician Proves That Prejudice Still Rules the Road," *The Washington Post,* August 16, 1998, C1.

[5] David Kocieniewski, "Study Suggests Racial Gap in Speeding in New Jersey," *The New York Times,* March 21, 2002.

In looking at crimes and traffic offenses more closely—and not just making *assumptions* based upon popular myths—the facts revealed that "black drivers" were actually the worst speeders. And then, as strange as it sounds, many of the critics, lawmakers, and "reformers" who were initially eager to publish the report suddenly claimed it was now "skewed" by problems with the methodology and now wanted the report withheld from publication:

> "When New Jersey officials prepared to release the report in January, Mark Posner, a lawyer with the Justice Department's special litigation section, asked the state attorney general's office to withhold it. Mr. Posner wrote that he feared that the report's results may have been skewed by factors like glare on windshields, weather and camera placements on roadsides."

Never mind that "glare on the windshields" would have prevented troopers from determining a driver's race in the first place, the statistics no longer supported the myth. In fact the more comprehensive study proved that "blacks" were actually the worst speeders—far beyond the threshold of so-called "demographic parity." And all the critics, legislators, and attorneys who couldn't wait for the study to be published, now wanted it to disappear. The news media seemed to follow along, and even though the New York Times revealed how officials and politicians in New Jersey got it wrong, the story still had a rather peculiar headline: "Study Suggests Racial Gap in Speeding In New Jersey."

Hopefully, this example illustrates why *assumptions* based upon statistics, no matter how ethical or important they may sound, hardly ring true. And hopefully, it also helps explain why Courageous Police Leaders must stay focused on the data—not the delusions—and challenge assumptions based upon statistics. Otherwise, if the assumptions aren't checked, there will likely be no end to the chaos and distractions they create for law enforcement. And without sticking to the facts, and statistics involving actual crimes and offenses, the law enforcement profession will remain stuck on the wrong side of the "slippery slope" of the "demographic parity" myth as well. After all, using statistics to support the myth of "demographic parity" is merely a convenience, but nonetheless arbitrary so far as actual crime is concerned. And that's where the problems start.

If we consider actual crime, does a law enforcement agency become racist if 15.1 percent of burglaries involve suspects of a particular demography that makes up only 15 percent of the population? Is there an acceptable gap between "demographic parity" and actual crime data and statistics? If so, who defines it and why? And at what point of "disparity" does a law enforcement agency automatically become racist?

Sure, speculating the "slippery slope," also known as the Sorites paradox, may be fun. However, many critics and law enforcement reformers manipulate statistics because they find it difficult, if not impossible, to provide actual evidence to otherwise support their often-outrageous claims. After all, it's much easier to bend statistics than provide actual evidence. And since many accusations based upon "demographic parity" tend to lack actual corroborative evidence, statistics get manipulated to fill in the blanks, and to create the illusion of vital facts and figures. But things go completely haywire whenever cowardly police leaders get involved.

Chaos in Los Angeles: The Problem with Politics and Good Police Work

For example, in 2015, Mayor Eric Garcetti doubled the size of LAPD's elite Metro Unit responsible for "responding to flare ups and tamping down gang wars" in Los Angeles.[6] However, after four years of effectively fighting crime, Mayor Garcetti ordered the LAPD to scale back its efforts in 2019, after a Los Angeles Times "investigative report" revealed an increase in the percentage of African-Americans stopped by LAPD Officers.[7] Of course, those who mistakenly believe in the myth of "demographic-parity" were "outraged" by the 7 percent increase from 21 to 28 percent. After all, African-Americans made up only 9 percent of the *overall population* of Los Angeles.

Aside from the obvious delusions, there's a lot of bending of statistics and data trickery going on here. In response to the "investigative report" and the "outrage," Mayor Garcetti ordered LAPD to "scale back" specifically on vehicle stops—which helped catch criminals and curtail problems in the most violent areas of Los Angeles. LAPD Chief Michel Moore admitted that the data could seem harsh. But he correctly pointed out how "intense policing is necessary in high-crime areas to keep residents safe," as he was quoted in the "investigative report." Chief Moore was also correct to point out that behind the demographic-parity nonsense are the actual victims of

---

[6] Cindy Chang, "L.A. Metro Cops Are in a Bind: Avoid Racial Profiling While Also Fighting Crime," *Los Angeles Times,* April 21, 2019.

[7] Cindy Chang and Ben Poston, "'Stop-and-Frisk in a Car:' Elite LAPD Unit Disproportionately Stopped Black Drivers, Data Show," *The Los Angeles Times,* January 24, 2019.

violence. However, using more specific data to explain the so-called disparity certainly would have helped.

And here's where the data trickery falls apart. As The Los Angeles Times "investigative report" points out, *the overall population* of African-Americans in Los Angeles is about 9 percent. However, the LAPD Metro Unit primarily focused its efforts in the most violent section of the city—South Los Angeles—where the African-American population is 24 percent. And just for reference, Hispanics make up 74 percent of the population of South Los Angeles, and Whites make up only about 1 percent.[8]

A more accurate comparison or "investigative report" would have indicated that so-called "minorities" make up 99 percent of the population—in the area where the Metro Unit was most active. However, this would undermine the myth of "demographic parity." Besides, the fact that 21 percent to 28 percent of the people stopped by the LAPD belong to a demographic group that represents 24 percent of population—where the most violent crimes occurred—doesn't make for such a shocking, investigative "revelation" or sensational headline. Although that doesn't stop the news media from conjuring up nonsense about the police stopping an unjust number of the "ethnic share of the city's residents"—whatever benchmark of misguided affirmative action that's supposed to be.[9]

[8] U.S. Census Bureau, *American Community Survey 1-year estimates*. Retrieved from *Census Reporter Profile page for Los Angeles County (South Central)—LA City (South Central/Watts) PUMA, CA*. (2017).

[9] Eric Leonard, "LAPD Chief Says It's Unclear Whether Race Complaints Linked to Crime Reduction," *NBC4 Los Angeles*, January 29, 2019.

Even if we permit the delusion of "demographic parity," using statistics about *the overall population* of Los Angeles is still misleading at the very least. And it's difficult to ignore how statistics weren't manipulated to better fit a narrative and a socio-political agenda. But again, none of this has to do with the reality of crime and criminal behavior. Violence was reduced in South Los Angeles after the Metro Unit initiative was put in place. And when Mayor Garcetti ordered the law enforcement efforts to stop, violence and shootings doubled in South Central Los Angeles.

But the absurdity and hypocrisy doesn't end there. Critics were complaining about "disproportionate" racial discrimination—ironically, in a neighborhood plagued by violent crime where "minorities" are the majority. And due to the complaints, Mayor Garcetti called for an audit.[10] Then he ordered the policing efforts to stop—and of course, violence spiked.[11] But when a local activist and rapper, who incidentally had reached out to the mayor to try and help stop the violence, was gunned down, Mayor Garcetti claimed he was "deeply concerned" about the violence.[12]

This is a textbook example of the vicious cycle of cowardly leadership, hypocrisy and the chaos that myths, lies, and misbeliefs about "demographic parity" can bring about. Granted this could span several years, if not

---

[10] Cindy Chang, "L.A. Mayor Garcetti Calls For Audit of Elite LAPD Unit Over Stops of Black Drivers," *Los Angeles Times,* January 29, 2019.

[11] Elliot McLaughlin, "Nipsey Hussle Slaying: From Street Gangs to Police and Lawmakers, Tributes Continue to Pour in," *CNN,* April 8, 2019.

[12] Marissa Wenzke and Ellina Abovian, "After Nipsey Hussle's Killing, LAPD Reports Spike in Gun Violence in South L.A.," *KTLA 5,* April 2, 2019.

decades. But in this case, it transpired all within the tenure of one particular mayor. This example should make it absolutely clear why Courageous Police Leaders must focus on facts, accurate data, and effective crime-fighting—and not give into myths and manipulated statistics.

This is necessary to not only protect the law enforcement profession, but ultimately the people who matter most: the victims, and the people who are suffering from inescapable crime and violence. Children and their parents don't care about statistics, they want to be safe—that's what really matters. And the more Courageous Police Leaders can get others to focus on what really matters—instead of politics, or pandering, or bending statistics for the sake of myths—the more likely real progress can be made.

COMBATING DATA-DRIVEN CHAOS

This example also points out another tactic that the enemies of law enforcement love to use whenever they obsess upon tiny pieces of data to "reveal" or "support" who-knows-what kind of far-fetched accusation. Granted, there are plenty of enemies of law enforcement who manipulate statistics in all sorts of ways. But one the most vocal critics—with some of the most predictable strategies and tactics—is the ACLU and its "follow-along" state chapters. Like the critics of the LAPD, an often-used tactic of the ACLU and its chapters seems to involve making a big deal out of "isolated" statistics to support popular anti-police sentiments.

NYPD "Stop & Frisk" Data

For example, in its analysis of annual NYPD stop-and-frisk data, the New York Civil Liberties Union (NYCLU) makes a bold claim: "Nearly nine out of 10 stop-and-frisked New Yorkers have been completely innocent."[13] It's a condemning assertion based on a tough-sounding statistic: "nine out of 10" or 90 percent were innocent. Plenty of cowardly leaders would run and hide if they faced such a statistic.

Although there's more to the story than that. The NYCLU claims that "nine out of 10" were innocent. However, the notes from their own analysis reveal several contradictions. For example, only about three out of four (76 percent) were actually innocent in 2016. And just two out of three (67 percent) were innocent in 2017. In fact, the NYCLU analysis indicates that the NYPD stopped fewer people overall—but encountered more "criminals," or fewer "innocent" people in recent years.

Obviously, the NYPD was doing a better job. But that doesn't seem to fit the story the NYCLU wants to tell. Although the same data used to fabricate a "shocking" statistic about the NYPD also shows they've made tremendous progress. Indeed, "averages" can be quite useful for creating slight-of-hand statistical illusions and nonsense. In looking at the actual data, the plummet in numbers between 2011 and 2014 is hard to miss. And whenever numbers rise steadily and then nose-dive, an *average* is going to be skewed, if not meaningless.

---

[13] Christopher Dunn and Michelle Shames, *Stop-and-frisk in the de Blasio Era,* New York: New York Civil Liberties Union, March 14, 2019. www.nyclu/SF2019

NYPD Stop & Frisks, 2002-2018

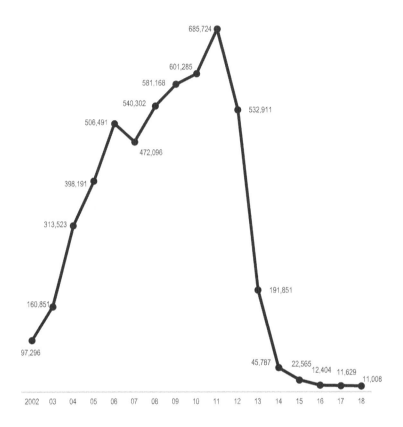

Figure 1. The number of stops and frisks conducted by the NYPD between 2002 and 2018, according to the NYCLU.

But hidden in the data is an important fact that the NYCLU fails to mention: between 2014 and 2018, the NYPD "stopped-and-frisked" fewer people—yet more of them were "not innocent."

YEAR	STOPS/FRISKS	NOT INNOCENT
2002	97,296	18%
2003	160,851	13%
2004	313,523	11%
2005	398,191	11%
2006	506,491	10%
2007	472,096	13%
2008	540,302	12%
2009	581,168	12%
2010	601,285	14%
2011	685,724	12%
2012	532,911	11%
2013	191,851	12%
2014	45,787	18%
2015	22,565	20%
2016	12,404	24%
2017	11,629	33%
2018	11,008	30%

Figure 2. The number of stops and frisks conducted by the NYPD between 2002 and 2018, and the number of "not innocent" persons that were encountered, according to the NYCLU.

So there are two undisputable facts that even the NYCLU's own data can't obscure:

1. The NYPD has become more effective; they're stopping-and-frisking fewer people, yet encountering more "not-innocent" people; and

2. The NYPD is arresting fewer criminals.

The first fact should be worthy of praise. The second should sound the alarm. Of course, if the NYCLU wants to re-write the "social contract" between cops and citizens, that's fine. But they should realize that sensational headlines that downplay commendable police efforts undermine the truth of the matter. And such tactics also undermine any cooperation toward making the very progress they seem so eager to make.

Being fair and giving due credit to the NYPD does not seem to be part of the NYCLU agenda, or a popular idea in general these days. But hopefully, it serves as an example of how critics and so-called "reformers" skew data and statistics. This isn't just messing around with numbers and averages—this is the kind of myth-making that undermines effective law enforcement, and denies giving praise and credit when it's hard earned and well deserved.

The Washington Post Police Shooting Database

Unfortunately, the ACLU and its state chapters aren't the only organizations that attempt to manipulate data and statistics to criticize law enforcement. Of course, news media outlets and social media pundits do the same. While there are thousands of examples, the Washington Post "Police Shooting Database"—and the multitude of news stories that reference it—provide a good example of the kind of chaos that Courageous Police Leaders may often encounter.

Since 2015, The Washington Post has kept a database of "civilians" shot and killed by police officers on duty.[14] However, buried in its description of the database, The Washington Post explains:

> "The Post is documenting only those shootings in which a police officer, in the line of duty, shoots and kills a civilian—the circumstances that most closely parallel the 2014 killing of Michael Brown in Ferguson, Mo.,"

While this says a lot about data research and media bias, the actual data itself tells a much different story. For example, according to the database, 992 people were shot and killed by police in 2018. It's a number that has not varied much since the data was first compiled in 2015.

---

[14] Julie Tate, Jennifer Jenkins, and Steven Rich, "Fatal Force: 2018 Police Shooting Database," *The Washington Post*, 2019: http://wapo.st/police-shootings-2018

YEAR	NUMBER OF SHOOTING FATALITIES
2018	992
2017	987
2016	963
2015	995

Figure 3. The number of shooting fatalities that occurred between 2015-2018, according to the Washington Post "Police Shootings Database."

Yet with all of the media and social media attention given to race-based social "justice" movements, and with all the racially focused news stories, one might expect that a disproportionate number of "blacks" were shot and killed by police. However, the actual data indicates a much different story.

RACE	NUMBER OF SHOOTING FATALITIES, 2018
"White"	452
"Black"	229
"Hispanic"	164
"Other"	40

Figure 4. The number of shooting fatalities in 2018 by race, according to the Washington Post "Police Shootings Database."

Clearly, in 2018 law enforcement shot and killed far more "White" people (452)—than all the other races combined (433). This isn't just an anomaly or random statistic, since practically the same number of shootings occurred in 2017 as well.

RACE	NUMBER OF SHOOTING FATALITIES, 2017
"White"	457
"Black"	223
"Hispanic"	179
"Other"	44

Figure 5. The number of shooting fatalities in 2017 by race, according to the Washington Post "Police Shootings Database."

The data and statistics indicate that significantly more "Whites" have been killed by law enforcement. However, that didn't stop The Washington Post, from publishing an article on March 16, 2018 with the pleading headline: "Police are still killing black people. Why isn't it news anymore?"[15]

Let's put the obvious media bias and readership pandering aside, and offer the benefit of the doubt. Yet what's so remarkable isn't what the Washington Post article says—but what it does not say. Of course, the article makes no mention of the dangerous crimes, behaviors, or outright deadly attempts that

---

[15] Wesley Lowery, "Police Are Still Killing Black People. Why Isn't It News Anymore?" *The Washington Post*, March 26, 2018.

any of the "victims" were engaged in which prompted the use of deadly force by law enforcement officers.

And for whatever reason, the article does not mention the worn-out, completely fabricated statistical claim that many other articles from the Washington Post repeat over and over again: "Black people are 2.5 times more likely to be shot dead by police."[16] Again, where's the connection, the statistical correlation between "Black people" and the crimes committed by "Black people" or any other race? And where's the explanation about the disconnect between "likelihood" and reality?

Every Courageous Police Leader should be wary of—if not ready to pounce upon—any statistical claim dealing with "likelihood." Attempts to suggest what *may likely happen,* must be thwarted for no other reason than they often grossly mispresent what *actually happened.* And at the very least, Courageous Police Leaders should recognize and point out that although social justice "warriors" may claim *likelihood matters,* "likelihood" hardly reflects the reality of crime or law enforcement—or the actual outcome of law enforcement efforts. Again, the most important statistic involving law enforcement is crime.

Indeed, "likelihood" and probability have nothing to do with the actual circumstances and outcomes of criminal behavior and law enforcement. And that's probably why manipulating statistics has become necessary for social justice "warriors," the media, and police "reformers." The *actual number* of

---

[16] Kimberly Kindy, Wesley Lowery, et al., "Fatal Shootings by Police Are Up in The First Six Months of 2016, Post Analysis Finds," *The Washington Post,* July 7, 2016.

people shot and killed by police according to race doesn't seem to fit too well with the "police are still killing black people" narrative. Shifting to "likelihood," however, offers a far more dramatic-sounding statistic. But it's still nonsense. Although mixing up statistics and probability sounds a lot better for fear-mongering and hurling broad accusations at law enforcement.

Fortunately, the statistical delusions of activists and police reformers can be easily debunked, as Harvard economist, Roland Fryer, Jr. has done. Fryer, an African-American, self-admitted former McDonald's (drive-thru) employee, didn't like cops growing up. This is partly because his family sold crack cocaine when he was younger. For these and plenty of other reasons, Fryer is probably the last person the media and social justice "warriors" would want questioning their "stylized facts" or pointing out how their "descriptive statistics, while poignant, do not prove racial bias."[17]

As part of his own research, Fryer studied police shootings involving the Houston Police Department. After gathering and analyzing data, Fryer concluded that "blacks are 27.4 percent *less likely* to be shot at by police relative to non-black, non-Hispanics." In other words, Fryer evidenced a factual contradiction: "blacks" are less likely to be shot at by the Houston PD.[18] At the same time, he also exposed something that social justice "warriors" and police "reformers" will likely never admit: statistical averages don't necessarily apply to specific regions, jurisdictions,

---

[17] Ronald G. Fryer, Jr., "Reconciling Results on Racial Differences in Police Shootings," *The National Bureau of Economic Research*, Working Paper No. 24238, January 2018.

[18] Max Ehrenfruend and Jeff Guo, "How a Controversial Study Found That Police Are More Likely to Shoot Whites, Not Blacks," *The Washington Post*, July 13, 2016.

communities, or neighborhoods: crime and criminal behavior could be better or worse in any particular place to the next. And extracting statistics and averages "to prove" something makes absolutely no sense when it comes to the circumstances of crime and criminal behavior—or law enforcement efforts in response to them.

Hopefully, these examples show some of the data deceptions and statistical myth-making that the enemies of law enforcement perpetrate. And hopefully it also explains why it's absolutely critical for Courageous Police Leaders to counter the chaos that often results from skewed data and statistics. Otherwise, every sensational headline, and every "startling statistic" will continue to corrupt public perception. And every time statistical trickery goes unchecked, it makes accusing and scapegoating law enforcement even easier, more rewarding—and somehow even more righteous.

FIGHT BACK AGAINST
MYTHS & MISINFORMATION

It may sound harsh to say that "news media" and "misinformation" are synonyms, as far as law enforcement professionals are concerned. It's not a light-hearted remark by any means, especially considering how the news media and law enforcement depend on each other in many ways. And it could easily be mistaken as a slap in the face for the many pro-law enforcement journalists and publications across the country. But with all the "mercenary critics," and brainwashed journalists who follow slanted and skewed editorial agendas against law enforcement, we shouldn't be kidding ourselves. And we shouldn't dismiss the challenges and chaos that less-than-accurate news reporting, misinformation, and bad publicity often create.

Following popular political trends, the news media has become increasingly critical of law enforcement. What used to be an exaggeration or editorial "oversight" has now become immediate cause for "outrage." And what was once effective criticism, is now a reason for protesting against law enforcement. And when a Twitter post and a bunch of hashtags can launch a national "movement," we ought to be concerned—very concerned.

However, misinformation and media bias has not only become increasingly inflammatory, it's become increasingly dangerous—and in some cases, even deadly. Of course, we could just chalk it up to the notion that American society has become less civil, or politically unhinged, or brainwashed by fake news and social media, or whatever else depending upon how far you care to let conspiracy theories play out. To a varying degree, the news media is partly to blame. Cowardly police leaders on the other hand, bear most of the blame, because they're the ones who've failed to correct factual inaccuracies and untruths in news and social media. Moreover, cowardly leaders are the ones who have allowed the ensuing chaos to harm the law enforcement profession and confuse and endanger the American public. Cowards are also in a position to know better: they know the difference between the actual facts and circumstances concerning law enforcement—and they know how they've been manipulated or misrepresented in the media. Yet they typically do nothing when the news media or social media get it all wrong.

Also, cowardly leaders typically fail to take a proactive approach toward news media. They'll try to get all the publicity they can for themselves. But in general, they tend to wait for inquiries from the media, and then react. That is, if they even respond at all. And when they do, instead of being clear, consistent, and deliberate, they often bend toward whatever they think people want to hear. And perhaps worst of all, they often avoid challenging media bias, and often bury their heads in the sand even when the most outlandish inaccuracies and accusations have been put out as "news."

Needless to say, Courageous Police Leaders must put a stop to all of this nonsense. If cowards typically *react* to media requests and rarely attempt to communicate more directly with the public, and bend to the demands of the media and popular approval, then Courageous Police Leaders must do the opposite—so that nobody has to suffer misinformation and the ensuing chaos, which can sometimes get officers killed.

FAKE NEWS: AN OFFICER SAFETY THREAT

Indeed, misinformation in the media can be deadly—and that's not an exaggeration. For example, the FBI Assailant Study analyzed cop killers and their frame of mind before they killed a police officer. Accordingly, 28 percent of cop killers said they planned to kill law enforcement officers for "social and/or political reasons." There's hardly anything shocking there. Yet, the same 28 percent also shared their beliefs and intentions on social media or with friends and family before ambushing or attacking law enforcement officers.[19] However, the study revealed something far more chilling about these cop killers:

> "These assailants expressed that they were distrustful of the police due to previous personal interactions with law enforcement *and what they heard and read in the media* about other incidents involving law enforcement shootings."[20]

The study also found that:

> "assailants were constantly exposed to a singular narrative by news organizations and social media of police misconduct and wrong-doing."

---

[19]"The Assailant Study- Mindsets and Behaviors," United States Department of Justice, Federal Bureau of Investigation.
[20] FBI Assailant Study; emphasis added.

If that's not convincing enough that a proactive response to news media is absolutely necessary for safety and survival, then consider another key finding of the FBI study:

> "...without law enforcement and elected officials providing an alternative narrative, assailants developed a distrust of law enforcement, and felt emboldened and justified in using violence against police."[21]

So let's be *absolutely clear.* By not challenging lies, myths, and inaccuracies in news media and social media, cowardly police leaders are enabling factors that could endanger the public and law enforcement personnel. And by avoiding conflict, cowards are validating if not encouraging anti-police sentiments, to some extent at the very least. This too was explained in the FBI Assailant Study:

> "Nearly every police official interviewed agreed that for the first time, law enforcement not only felt that their national political leaders [publicly] stood against them, but also that the politicians' words and actions signified that disrespect to law enforcement was acceptable in the aftermath of the Brown shooting."

And since the news media is a key distributor of the "politicians' words and actions" and bringing them to the attention of the public—and cop assailants—hopefully it's clear to see why Courageous Police Leaders must do more to combat cowardly leadership, and the misinformation they permit in the news, and all the chaos that often results.

---

[21] FBI Assailant Study, page 3.

A PROACTIVE APPROACH TO NEWS MEDIA

As a profession, law enforcement has been slow in taking up a more direct, proactive approach. It's crazy to think that law enforcement can control everything in the media all the time. But it's just as crazy to let news media and social media be the only voices and the only sources of news and information regarding law enforcement activities. Ideally, every law enforcement agency should have its own voice in public conversations about law enforcement, to whatever extent that's necessary and practical.

Fortunately, more and more Courageous Police Leaders are catching on, and taking a more proactive approach. For example, Prince George (Maryland) County Police Chief Hank Stawinski abides by what he calls the "three-hour rule." Within three hours after a critical incident, or as soon as physically possible, he gets in front of a camera and explains the incident to the public. According to Chief Stawinski:

> "If you wait 72 hours, or 10 days, people are going to fill in the blanks and draw their own conclusions. Once that happens, no matter what you say, no matter how you say it, the truth will never be properly accepted…"[22]

And he doesn't just talk the talk. In September 2018, Chief Stawinski stood before the media to confront demands for information about how officers under his command served a search warrant at the wrong address after being misinformed, and got into a shoot-out with a "law-abiding citizen" who had nothing to do with the warrant. In the news conference, Chief

---

[22] Tom Jackman, "Prince George's Police Chief Does Amazing Thing: Provides Facts and Apologizes For a Mistake Almost Immediately," *The Washington Post*, September 24, 2018.

Stawinski explained the facts that he had at the time. He apologized to the public, and apologized to the man who mistakenly shot at police officers serving the warrant, and vowed to do everything he could to prevent such mistakes from happening again.

Chief Stawinski could have ignored the media requests. And he could have blamed others or bent the truth. But unlike cowardly police leaders, Chief Stawinski faced the media and faced the facts. And he demonstrated how the integrity and quick action of a courageous police chief not only set the tone — but set the record straight — and helped quell the unrest in his community.

There's another reason why being proactive, if not being first to publish information, may be absolutely necessary. Much like the early bird that catches the worm, those who tell the story first gain an advantage. The first story is usually the one that gets remembered, or at least, becomes the first point of reference for other stories that follow. And as Chief Stawinski pointed out, if you wait too long, it doesn't matter what the facts are, or how you explain them, people aren't going to accept them, or they'll remain skeptical at the least. So why not be first? After all, law enforcement agencies can publish and share information on many of the same social media platforms that traditional news outlets use.

Another reason to be first to publish information is that it can provide the advantage of explaining the facts and circumstances before lies and myths run wild — which is what happened with the "Hands Up, Don't Shoot" myth that began in Ferguson. So why do so many people believe the misinformation? The answer is simple: the "Hands Up, Don't Shoot" myth came first — and cowardly leaders did nothing to initially dispel the lies.

And once lies transform into "outrage" and demands for "justice," facts hardly matter anymore.

If it sounds like we're advocating that law enforcement agencies act as their own media outlet, that's exactly right. It's what every law enforcement agency should do, practically speaking. And by being proactive, or being first to deliver factually accurate information, Courageous Police Leaders can do a lot to prevent misinformation and misunderstanding—and prevent a whole lot of unnecessary chaos.

While improving public relations and creating media can be done with a smartphone, it may still seem overwhelming and complicated for some agencies. However, to combat the chaos and the dangerous consequences that misinformation can bring about, every law enforcement agency should commit to at least one thing: not letting lies and myths go unchecked without a response.

We're not talking about proofreading everything in the newspaper or tracking every social media post. We're talking about responding to the big stuff, and offering perspective to myths and misinformation that create chaos and embolden cop killers, as the FBI Assailant Study suggests. So, when protesters swarm the parking lot, or rocks are flying in the streets, or an attorney is about to read a statement "on behalf of the family," it's not the time to ignore controversy—it's time to be courageous and respond.

USE VIDEO TO COMBAT CHAOS
(NOT CREATE IT)

"If you have nothing to hide you have nothing to fear."
—Upton Sinclair

Fortunately, we've come a long way since the early '90s, when box-like video cameras took up the dashboard and VCRs basically made the trunk useless. However, while video and bodycam technology has improved tremendously, it seems we've gone backwards in how we use video for the benefit of law enforcement.

HAVE NOTHING TO HIDE

With all the scrutiny and never-ending demands for "transparency," far too many cowardly police leaders are mishandling video in one way or another. However, taking a timely, "nothing to hide" approach to law enforcement video offers several advantages. For one thing, taking a "nothing to hide" approach and pro-actively publishing or granting access to law enforcement video—by default—can drastically help reduce suspicion of wrongdoing.

Secondly, delaying the release of video won't eliminate the inevitable. If the video depicts unbecoming conduct or misconduct, it's best to deal with it sooner rather than later. And while the content of a video may be problematic, a timely "nothing to hide" approach may help prevent things from getting worse, and may even provide an advantage toward influencing public response.

Lastly, aside from showing how officers react and behave, releasing a video can also help reveal the lies and false accusations of less-than-truthful citizens as well. Which can go a long way to help the public better understand law enforcement practices, especially since videos showing the lies and false complaints against law enforcement personnel are hardly used for the maximum advantage they can provide.

Sure, everybody knows that people lie to the police. However, releasing videos that show what "really happened" can certainly help cut down false accusations and fabricated complaints—and ironically, help improve public relations overall. The point of releasing such videos isn't about embarrassing anyone; it's about matter-of-factly showing the lies and nonsense that law enforcement must deal with when false accusations fly.

For example, a reverend and local NAACP President filed a complaint because he was subjected to racial discrimination during a traffic stop involving a Timmonsville (South Carolina) Police Officer in June 2018. The accusations were awful—the kind that no leader ever wants to hear about, and no officer wants to be put up against. The reverend/NAACP president explained in detail how he had been "racially profiled" on Facebook. And it didn't take long before a community activist showed up at the police station demanding to see the bodycam video of the traffic stop.

Timmonsville Police Chief Billy Brown immediately obliged the activist's request to see the video. And after watching the bodycam footage, the activist was absolutely floored. However, it wasn't the alleged "racial profiling" that he found so shocking—it was the fact that the reverend/NAACP President lied about practically everything.

When asked about the video, the activist replied, "Once I got a copy of that body cam, it's as if he [the reverend/NAACP President] made the whole story up." And after releasing the video of the traffic stop—to quell the discontent that had already began to simmer thanks to the Facebook post—Chief Brown also expressed his concerns:

> "When I saw the video, I was shocked that someone who is supposed to be a community leader, a pastor, and head of the NAACP would just come out and tell a blatant lie. It bothered me. It really bothered me, thinking about the racial unrest it could've caused in the community and it's just troubling to me that someone who held a position like that would come out and just tell a lie."[23]

And in speaking of the importance of the video, Chief Brown also explained:

> The video tells everything. [...] The video tells you who, what he claimed happened and what didn't happen.

Of course, there is no shortage of liars and people who lie to the police—and people who make false accusations against law enforcement officers. Chief Brown's quick action and pro-active release of the bodycam video put the truth on display, which helped spare him, his department, and his officers from becoming embroiled in racial strife—all because of a lie.

Likewise, Courageous Police Leaders would be wise to do the same. That is, release videos involving complaints *proactively*. There's no reason to wait until activists are pounding on the door. This approach can help dispel the accusations and lies, and also help prevent them from happening again

---

[23] Larry Elder, "Black Motorists Lying: Who's Doing 'Racial Profiling'?" *The Courier-Tribune,* June 12, 2018.

because once people catch on that police videos involving their "complaints" will be made available publicly, they may think twice, which may help cut down on bogus accusations and outright lies.

Of course, whether a video shows a citizen lying, or alleged police misconduct, there may be times when releasing law enforcement video may compromise an investigation or public safety. In these instances, it's best to release at least something—even just a snippet—along with an explanation of the circumstances. This can help alleviate the pressure and promote at least some understanding about why the rest of the video cannot be released at the moment. Releasing something is better than nothing—because "nothing" typically allows contempt and chaos to fester.

Of course, chaos often involves political pressure. Which is probably why there's a growing trend to require law enforcement agencies to release videos within a certain time-frame after a deadly use-of-force incident. For example, in Connecticut, the state legislature recently passed a bill requiring police departments to release videos from dash cams and body cams within 96 hours after an incident has occurred.[24]

RELEASING VIDEO—WITH CONTEXT

However, releasing a video in a timely manner is one thing—explaining it is another. In fact, releasing a video without any context or explanation can often cause more harm than good. Simply put, without context, there's likely to be chaos. But releasing a video with context and explanation can help

---

[24] Kelan Lyons and Maya Moore, "House Passes Police Accountability Bill Over Republican Objections," *CT Mirror*, June 5, 2019.

tremendously, and help everyone better understand the context, circumstances, and decision-making involved.

For example, when Cottonwood (Arizona) Police arrived at a Wal-Mart after an employee was assaulted on March 21, 2015, they had no idea what was about to unfold. Ultimately, eight officers, nine suspects, and a Walmart employee were involved in a violent brawl. One of the suspects was struggling to get an officer's gun, prompting the officer to respond with deadly force.

The next day, news headlines across the country claimed that Cottonwood Police officers shot and killed an unarmed "Christian band member." Needless to say, the headlines significantly distorted the truth, and releasing a video of the brawl would help set the record straight. But Chief Fanning was told by the investigative agency that the video was evidence and therefore, could not be released.

Chief Fanning had a difficult decision to make. Not releasing the video would allow the lies to keep spreading out of control. And releasing the video would certainly put his employment at risk. Despite the challenges, Chief Fanning made a courageous choice. He scheduled a press conference to release and explain the video. Of course, news stations asked him to just email it, but Fanning knew better. He refused such requests, and told reporters that if they wanted a copy of the video, they must attend the news conference.

Chief Fanning did something else quite remarkable. He played the eight-minute video in real-time—and then gave a detailed, practically frame-by-frame explanation, so news personnel could better understand what was going on in the video. During the slow-motion playback, Chief Fanning paused at key moments to explain the actions and the decisions the officers made—in response to the threats, physical harm, and imminent dangers they faced. It took about an hour, but Fanning left no doubt about why the officers used deadly force.

Chief Fanning's efforts are nothing but commendable. He made a tough choice and provided clear explanations in the context of the video. We could say this was remarkable, but it would be even better to say it's just routine, because this should be routine—and not only when controversy arises. Routinely publishing law enforcement videos with context and explanation can help pre-empt controversies, misunderstandings, and chaos in the first place.

Similarly, the Los Angeles Police Department (LAPD) provides a good model for releasing a video recording, and how to provide context to prevent misunderstandings. They provide background about the call or incident, along with detailed explanations of what transpired. The video is then presented—along with key details such as, "You will see in this freeze frame a handgun..."

In discussing the LAPD approach to releasing videos, LAPD Commission President Steve Soboroff stated:

> "I don't believe, the way the others have done it, that you learn anything about policing. These [video] releases are to put out facts, one way or the other, but they are also to show the context of these one one-hundredth of a second decisions."[25]

And that's something every Courageous Police Leader should bear in mind when it comes to releasing videos and combating chaos.

USING VIDEO FOR A DIFFERENT PERSPECTIVE

Nothing could be more cowardly than releasing videos of use-of-force incidents—and not releasing videos about other aspects of law enforcement. In fact, you can spot a law enforcement agency suffering from cowardly leadership when the only videos they have available involve use of force— which happens whenever agencies only *respond* to video requests instead of taking a more proactive approach. Aside from misrepresenting the law enforcement profession to the general public, it's a great disservice to the men and women behind the badge. And especially so, considering that more than 99 percent of law enforcement interactions do not involve the use of force.[26] Indeed, releasing videos showing the other aspects of law enforcement can help change misperceptions and counter one-sided narratives, and help counter how cowards misuse videos.

---

[25] James Queally, "LAPD Hopes New Video Policy Can Turn Dangerous Clashes Into Teachable Moments," *Los Angeles Times,* June 29, 2018.

[26] "Police Use of Force in America," International Association of Chiefs of Police, 2001: ii.

HOW COWARDS MISUSE VIDEO

Without a doubt, the cowards among us are misusing videos as a way to throw officers under the bus. One of the most damaging ways involves denying officers from reviewing videos *before* they write a report. And making matters worse, they're putting policies in place that put officers' words and recollections up against video recordings. Let's call this what it is: a set-up to blame officers whenever their written reports do not "match" what's depicted in a video. Why else would cowardly leaders insist upon "write first/watch second" policies and procedures? And why else would they deny officers access to videos before they complete their reports?

Granted, there are times when this may be necessary. But as normal protocol, the "write first/watch second" approach undermines trust and destroys morale. And it opens the door for all kinds of unnecessary scrutiny — including the vile scrutiny that only a defense attorney could conjure.

Denying officers video review basically sets up a "game over before the game even begins" scenario. And "write first, watch second" policies do little else but breed inconsistencies and inspire second-guessing. Even the slightest discrepancies between a written report and a recorded video can become unnecessary sticking points — if not a reason for a juror to doubt everything officers have to offer in their testimony. And considering how the criminal justice system is tempered by reasonable doubt, cowardly leaders are setting up plenty of doubt — before the case even hits a prosecutor's desk — by not allowing officers to review videos before writing their reports.

This accomplishes little more than the manufacturing of "versions" of an incident—and plenty of doubt and suspicion. Video will show one thing—and of course, an officer's perspective, recollection, and perception will differ. Why would anyone expect anything else?

Honestly, there is one particular reason that can explain why cowardly leaders, and social justice "warriors" and their ally attorneys want to deny officers from reviewing video recordings: to prosecute them. Case law has established sensible doctrines and standards that help protect law enforcement officers in doing their jobs. These are formidable obstacles for the so-called police "reformers" and social justice "warriors" who crave instant gratification. So it's a whole lot easier to manufacture doubt from the get-go and subsequently charge officers for supposed "acts of perjury." And whenever "reformers," policy advocates, and watchdog groups consider it a good thing that officers are prohibited from viewing video *before* they write a report, the writing is on the wall—and chaos is right around the corner.[27]

The so-called watch-dogs, the "reformers," and social justice "warriors" don't seem to understand that if a video shows officer misconduct, nothing can explain that away. And any attempt to do so will only underscore the misconduct, which is exactly what happened in the Walter Scott case. If an officer did something wrong, the video will provide all that's necessary for "accountability" and "transparency."

So here's the upshot: cowardly police leaders are trying way too hard to appease "reformers," police oversight committees, and political agendas.

---

[27] For example, see the ""Policy Body Worn Cameras: A Policy Scorecard,"," *The Leadership Conference on Civil and Human Rights & Upturn.* https://www.bwcscorecard.org.

And by demanding that officers file a report without being able to review any video, they're not only setting up officers for failure—they're undermining the entire criminal justice system with policies and procedures that manufacture doubt.

And let's not forget the reality of it all. "Discrepancies" between an officer's written report and a video recording create doubt to let criminals off the hook, much to the delight of defense attorneys everywhere. This can lead to plenty of complications in an already overburdened system of justice. And needless to say, it opens up a new frontier of misunderstanding and misjudgment among police oversight committees and review boards. To sum it all up, the cowardly handling of law enforcement video will likely bring about more and more chaos. Unless of course, Courageous Police Leaders step up and do something about it—and enact policies and procedures that make better use of video and body cam footage to help law enforcement efforts, not hinder them.

Courageous Police Leaders will proactively release videos showing a wide variety of police activities.

POLICE WITH A PLAN

"Ponder and deliberate before you make a move..."
—*Sun Tzu*

If video recordings can explain *what happened,* then policing plans can explain *what will happen* when law enforcement officers must take action. The fact that cowardly leaders often bungle communicating with the public is hardly surprising. But the number of law enforcement agencies that operate without a policing plan to help them communicate is in many ways even more surprising.

Basically, a policing plan is quite like a business plan—something that smart business leaders use to plan and successfully run their businesses. Likewise, Courageous Police Leaders use policing plans to run their departments, their precincts, or their squads more effectively—with better communication and fewer misunderstandings within the communities they serve.

CHASE AWAY THE COWARDS

Whenever police departments operate without a policing plan, cowardly leaders are given free range. Obviously, being able to act on a whim, or get away with knee-jerk reactions can cause all kinds of problems. However, policing plans make it difficult for cowardly leaders to just *react.* Instead, they're expected to *respond* according to a plan, which helps make their cowardly behavior stick out like a sore thumb. At the very least, a policing plan gives officers and the public a point of reference for better results—and better police leadership.

PLANS ARE NOT POLICIES

For clarity, a policy is one thing; and a plan is another. That is, policies and procedures focus on explaining *what* to do and *how* to do it. While policing plans explain *why* a department and its officers do what they do, and *how* their actions align with achieving specific goals and objectives. Or another way of thinking about it is this: a policy provides direction for officers; and a policing plan provides an explanation for the public.

For example, a good policing plan should explain *why* your department issues more warnings instead of traffic citations, or the other way around if that's the case. Or it should explain *why* a zero-tolerance policy regarding a particular crime has been enacted. Or *why* officers will be stepping up particular law enforcement efforts in certain (high-crime) areas. Policing plans are also a good opportunity to inform and educate the public about *why* officers use certain tactics or equipment.

And just like a sound business plan, policing plans should be updated on a regular basis as the mission, goals, or circumstances change within the agency. For example, the Sand Springs (Oklahoma) Police Department has an outstanding Policing Plan.[28] It is updated annually, provides clear explanations, and even shows how their reasons and decisions align with national standards.

---

[28] Sand Springs Police Department, "Policing Plan 2019," 2019. See also, http://sandspringsok.org

Here's an excerpt from their plan about the use of thermal-imaging cameras:

3.11 - Thermal Imaging Cameras on Patrol Units

The City of Sand Springs' greatest crime problem revolves around property theft. Burglary of automobiles sets the bar in this category and is one of the most difficult crimes to solve. Suspects involved in these cases tend to use darkness as a way to avoid detection and to escape when caught in the act. Our agency has found a tool that we believe will help us to mitigate that trend and bring suspects into custody. We will be equipping 15 of our patrol units with the Noptic NV3 thermal imaging system that will allow our officer to detect the heat signature of prowlers, burglars and others that use the night time to their advantage. We hope this will lessen the frustration of our citizens by reducing the amount of criminal activity in the area. This system cannot see into homes and will be used in accordance within the guidelines set forth by court case law.
(Exceeds the recommendations of the *President's Task Force on 21st Century Policing*).

Notice how this explanation has nothing to do with procedures. Instead, it explains *why* the Sands Springs PD plan to use thermal-imaging cameras. It also explains *how* the technology relates to targeting burglaries and giving criminals fewer places to hide. It also addresses one of the key concerns that citizens voiced about thermal-imaging technology. These are the kinds of explanations that should be a part of every effective policing plan.

Another excerpt explains why all Sand Springs PD patrol vehicles are equipped with tire-deflation units:

3.5 - Pursuit Termination Options

The Sand Springs Police Department is committed to using technology to reduce the risk of harm to citizens, officers, and suspects during pursuit situations. Every patrol unit is equipped with a Stinger tire deflation unit to help end pursuits. Pursuits and the use of the tire deflation devices are governed by our Lexipol policy project. (Complies with the Final Report of the President's Task Force on 21st Century Policing recommendation 1.1, 3.1.3, 3.2 and 3.5).

These excerpts focus on technology and are part of the more comprehensive Sand Springs PD policing plan. Likewise, a comprehensive policing plan should explain technology and tactics, but also describe other critical law enforcement efforts, highlight significant crime problems, and define crime reduction goals—all of which can go a long way toward improving understanding and pre-empting chaos.

A Policing Plan may sound simplistic. But Courageous Police Leaders are well aware about how a decision they make today can affect their department in the future. So why discuss thermal imaging when nobody may seem to care? Because one day in the future, someone without much expertise—but a whole lot of "influence"—will decry how the department is spying on innocent citizens in their homes. And when this happens, the Courageous Police Leader can show the community how this issue was addressed long ago—and shut down the attempts to decry "injustice" or whatever the unfounded complaints may be.

DEVELOPING A POLICING PLAN

During our *Courageous Police Leadership* seminars, many participants ask, "What should we put in a policing plan?" Obviously, we can't tackle every problem every agency will face in the space within this book. So hopefully a more general answer will suffice. To get the most bang for your buck out of a policing plan, it's best to focus on the top crime problems in your community—and explain *why* your agency uses particular tactics and strategies to address them. It's also a good idea to focus on the most common questions and concerns of community members.

Some good starting points include answering questions about why your agency operates as it does during a crisis or critical event, for example, explaining how your agency handles officer-involved shootings the way that it does, or why different levels of force (in response to different kinds of threats) may be used. And why your agency is focused on somethings but seems to be ignoring others. Providing explanations with clear details in plain and simple terms can help citizens better understand your law enforcement efforts. And it can also help make attempts to question and criticize a law enforcement agency seem foolish.

Overall, the goal is to develop a policing plan that provides as many details as necessary so that few people will question why your agency did what it did during a critical incident, or why your department is focusing on a particular crime, or crime area. Granted, there'll always be somebody who questions everything. But the point is to have a plan—and follow the plan—so there's less confusion and chaos overall.

Lastly, it's worth remembering that law enforcement is a high-risk business. And when men and women are called to dangerous scenes, placed in high stress situations, and are confronted by dangerous individuals, the question isn't *if* a critical incident is going to happen, it's a matter of *when*. So when critical incidents occur, and the public demands answers and "justice," indeed there's a significant advantage in being able to point to a policing plan—with plenty of answers at the ready to help quell any confusion before it turns into chaos.

Policing plans enable an agency to explain their practices before any chaos may erupt following an incident.

TRAIN WITH COURAGE

> "Courage, above all things, is the first quality of a warrior."
> — *Karl von Clausewitz*

Training isn't something officers should have to fight for—especially since they must face the struggles and the consequences for the lack of it. But unfortunately, training has indeed become a battleground in the law enforcement profession. Granted, there will always be tough choices to make about the typical constraints, such as limited budgets, staffing, available downtime, etc. But when cowardly leaders use training like a carrot on a stick—as though learning to do a better job is a reward—there's something amiss in the law enforcement profession. When cowards demand that officers "pay their dues"—as though gaining skills and experience must be a struggle—there's something wrong. And when cowardly leaders and politicians keep citizens in the dark about how they're paying for law enforcement training—or the lack of it—one way or another, there is something fundamentally wrong.

THE PROBLEM WITH BARE-MINIMUM "MINIMUM STANDARDS"

In many ways, the greatest battles regarding training are won and lost according to the so-called "minimum standards." Of course we need someplace to start, a foundation, a baseline for the minimum skills and proficiency necessary to be certified as a law enforcement officer. However, the problem isn't the necessity of "minimum standards"—the problem is just how minimal the "minimum standards" are.

Having met with thousands of law enforcement professionals throughout the country over the years, we've met very few officers who said they were being adequately trained for the job they were expected to do. And that leads us to perhaps the biggest, most fundamental problem of them all: how state and municipal governments *do so little* to adequately provision and fund "legislatively mandated training" —yet *expect so much* from law enforcement officers.

Of course, the "minimum standards" typically require hundreds of hours of training to become a certified police officer. But there's something wrong with the bigger picture when state laws and regulations require more training to become a cosmetologist than a cop. According to the "minimum standards" in Nevada for example, 800 hours of training are required for certification as a police officer—but more than 1,200 are required to be a hair designer, and 1,800 hours are required to be a cosmetologist.[29]

---

[29] See respectively NEVADA STATUTE NAC § 289.025 (2018); and NRS § 644A.315, and 644A.300.

And it's the same in other states, which should seem truly alarming.

	POLICE OFFICER TRAINING HOURS	OTHER LICENSED TRAINING HOURS
California	664	1,600 Cosmetologist
Florida	770	1,760 Interior Designer
Louisiana	360	500 Manicurist
North Carolina	620	1,520 Barber

Figure 6. The "minimum" training hours required to become a licensed police officer; and the hours required for other professional licenses, in selected states.

Of course, plenty of law enforcement agencies provide a lot more training in their police academies, and yearly re-certification. But in general, cowardly police leaders—and cowardly politicians and legislators—have done tremendous damage to the law enforcement profession by allowing such minimal training requirements to be established in the first place, and allowing them to linger.

The "minimum standards" to *initially qualify* for certification must absolutely be improved. But the training required to *maintain certification* must also be improved. Quite frankly, the training required each year to maintain certification is perhaps the biggest joke of all. And once again we find cowardly leaders, politicians, and legislators being hypocrites. They're *really quick* to blame officers and a "lack of training" after high-profile incidents.

Yet they're *really slow* at providing funds to improve training and advance "minimum standards"—although that's hardly a laughing matter. Cutting through the chaos, improving police training is well within the hands of state legislators, as defined by their "legislative mandated training" requirements.

	YEARLY TRAINING HOURS REQUIRED	TRAINING DETERMINED BY
Alaska	0	Legislature
Hawaii	0	Legislature
Illinois	0	Legislature
New York	0	Legislature
Iowa	12	Legislature
West Virginia	16	Legislature
Nebraska	20	Legislature
New Mexico	20	Legislature
South Dakota	20	Legislature
California	24—every 2-year cycle	Legislature

Figure 7. The number of training hours required to maintain certification as a police officer in various states, and the state authority ultimately responsible for determining those requirements.

Indeed, in most states, the state legislature is responsible for determining the "minimum standards" and yearly training requirements to maintain certification. Some do a better job than others. Some are appalling. But all of them are problematic.

For example, only 12 hours of additional law enforcement training are required per year in California. Yes, in the most populated state in America, the legislature only requires about 12 hours of training per year. That alone is a problem. But it's even more of a problem considering how state legislators have done relatively little, if anything to improve "minimum standards." Yet *somehow* they've managed to fund "de-escalation" training and use-of-force training—which were both politically popular leading up to the 2019-2020 legislative session.[30]

PAYING THE PRICE FOR THE LACK OF TRAINING

However, there's a key difference between doing what's popular—and doing what's necessary. And thanks to little more than the bare minimum, and funding "hot topic" subjects while ignoring the rest, officers suffer from the lack of training they need—and tax-payers are paying the price. Officers must deal with the frustrations of not getting the training they need. But when they get plenty of other kinds of training, such as the politically popular "de-escalation" training, the imbalance can become not only frustrating, but deadly for law enforcement officers.

---

[30] Don Thompson, "California Senate Passes Police Use of Force Training Bill," *Associated Press*, May 28, 2019.

For example, in June 2019, a Sacramento (California) Police training officer and a rookie officer were trying to "de-escalate" a domestic-violence situation. But here's something that cowards, social justice "warriors," and politicians seem to forget: *criminals will do whatever they want to do*—and no amount of "de-escalation" is going to stop them. And this is precisely what happened in this case. The suspect ambushed Training Officer Daniel Chip and rookie Officer Tara O'Sullivan with a high-powered rifle. Tragically, O'Sullivan was shot and killed.

Ambushes are one of the most difficult situations for any officer to face. And whenever "de-escalation" training is out of balance with survival or other critical training aspects, officers can become disadvantaged.[31] Regrettably, as tragedies like this continue to mount in the law enforcement profession, the need for training that protects the lives of officers should intensify, least of all to help prevent officers from unnecessarily making the ultimate sacrifice.

Citizens and taxpayers are also paying the price, even if they don't know it. Municipal governments throughout America are paying thousands if not millions of dollars every year to settle lawsuits alleging police misconduct, excessive force, and other wrong-doings. Just for reference, they're not spending government dollars to settle these lawsuits; they're spending tax dollars. And in that regard, and in failing to prioritize law enforcement training, it seems our political leaders and legislators are not being good financial stewards.

---

[31] Ryan Sabalow, Phillip Reese, and Benjy Egel, "Police Departments Are Younger and Less Experienced. Why That Matters in the Field," *The Sacramento Bee,* June 21, 2019.

Think for a moment about how things could improve if lawmakers actually funded law enforcement training properly—instead of just funding "politically popular" training programs. What if a fraction of the millions of dollars paid to settle lawsuits—*and paid to attorneys for legal fees*—was invested in police training efforts up front? And what if these funds were used to improve "minimum standards" and improve yearly training requirements as well? Without a doubt, the level of expertise and professionalism in law enforcement would be elevated, which could help reduce lawsuits in the first place—and help save lives.

Granted, there's no way to mitigate every instance of police misconduct—or *supposed misconduct*. And nothing can completely insulate a law enforcement agency or municipal government from situations where things go wrong, even when police do everything right. However, the fact that funding law enforcement training is not a priority in general, or not part of a strategy to prevent lawsuits from happening in the first place, says quite a lot. And it speaks volumes considering how cowardly leaders seem to be ignoring the advice of leading experts in criminal justice finance, who typically suggest taking preventative steps to limit liability.

For example, David Eichenthal, the executive director of the PFM Center for Justice & Safety Finance explains:

"The ability to limit your future liability by taking preventive steps upfront isn't just good policing policy, but important financial policy."[32]

When Eichenthal and other leading experts advise that "it's better to prevent than to pay out," the lack of funding, the lack of prioritization for law enforcement training, and the disregard for bringing up the "minimum standards" among politicians and legislators should seem quite suspect. And even more so when legislators magically seem to make funding available for training in areas that are politically popular, while practically ignoring everything else when it comes to law enforcement training.

BETTER TRAINING: A BATTLE ON THREE FRONTS

To overcome these circumstances, Courageous Police Leaders can gain advantage by fighting for better training on three fronts, by:

1. *Building alliances with legislators and political leaders* who are willing to do what's "unpopular but necessary" to improve "minimum standards" and support better training for law enforcement officers;

2. *Ensuring every dollar available for training is spent wisely* on the most effective training possible.

3. *Defending training that officers need*—especially when the enemies attempt to mischaracterize it.

---

[32] Liz Farmer, "Police Misconduct Is Increasingly a Financial Issue," *Governing*, June 20, 2018; see also Daniel Feldman and David Eichenthal, *The Art of the Watchdog: Fighting Fraud, Waste, Abuse and Corruption in Government*, (Albany, New York: SUNY Excelsior Press, 2014).

Building alliances for better training

Gaining advantages on this front depends upon collaborating with legislators who are willing to fight on behalf of law enforcement. Despite all the chaos and how little attention they are given in the media, there are plenty of legislators out there who are sympathetic to the law enforcement profession. They understand how training can not only make a difference in professionalism—but also help reduce all kinds of problems. It's crucial to form alliances with those responsible for the jurisdiction of a particular law enforcement agency. But it's also important to form alliances with those whose influence spans farther beyond. Likewise, forming alliances which span different political levels, is also an excellent idea for ensuring that training and other key law enforcement issues are not only understood, but prioritized on various levels. Courageous Police Leaders would be wise to not only stress the need and importance of a particular training program— but clearly explain the risks and consequences of not provisioning such training as well.

Spending wisely to get the best training

Fighting for better training on the second front is a bit like waging war from within, so to speak. That's because even if legislators and politicians provide for all the training an agency could ever need, chances are, some cowardly leader will make a mess of even the most necessary and most straightforward training programs.

One of the ways that cowards most often undermine training and hold back the profession is through their insistence upon providing just enough training to "check the boxes." And in so doing, they often fail to provide the kinds of training that law enforcement professionals need to survive and thrive—whether it's a legal battle or a gun battle. However, aside from "checking the boxes" and doing the bare minimum, cowards have increasingly become out of touch with the kinds of training that officers need the most. And they mistakenly believe that *any* training program will suffice—and the cheaper, the better. Cowards tend not to care about content, quality, or gaining proficiency. They seem more concerned with "getting through" training so they can "check the boxes."

The challenge here is getting cowards to understand that when it comes to effective training, quality counts. They must understand how getting the best training, from the best instructors, and the best means can make a tremendous difference—the difference between training that gets put to good use—and training that is basically forgotten before the course is even over. And it's not about spending top dollar. It's about combating and undoing the "check the boxes" mentality, and "the cheaper the better" approach that cowards often take toward training budgets. It's also about establishing a more investment-like strategy toward law enforcement training. Because that's exactly what training is—an investment in the knowledge, skills, and professionalism of an agency and its officers. And good training pays dividends, least of all by helping to keep both officers and the public safe.

Defending training—even against the absurd

For the most part, public safety hasn't been a top priority for most legislators and politicians. Sure, they'll make all sorts of claims, yet they rarely follow through. Of course there are exceptions, but for the most part, law enforcement training—the kinds that officers need most—is an afterthought. That's if it's given any thought at all. Along with the abominable "minimum standards," terrible yearly training requirements, and "check-the-box" laziness and misspending, there's another critical front that demands courageous leadership.

Thanks to the popularity of "political correctness," cowardly police leaders and politicians are re-defining training programs to appease social justice "warriors" and so-called police "reformers." And they're increasingly misinterpreting—and often flat out misunderstanding—the training that officers need most. Consequently, the struggle to improve law enforcement training has in many ways become a war of words.

For example, while cowards seem all too eager to take advice from social justice "warriors"—they seem to be ignoring how in the worst of situations, *true warriors* are needed. Or what else should we call the brave men and women in uniform who are expected to run into schools with an active shooter on the loose? Or those who run toward danger to selflessly save the lives of others? Or those on duty who are first on scene of unspeakable tragedies, and are expected to handle the next call as though nothing happened?

There are many befitting words for the everyday heroes of law enforcement—and *warrior* is one of them. It's been used to describe similar acts and behavior for centuries. However, since being judgmental is trendy nowadays, cowardly leaders seem to be doing everything possible to avoid using the term *warrior* since it's "inappropriate" and too "offensive" for the politically correct crowd.

Avoiding the word *warrior* is one thing, but avoiding "warrior-like" training is something completely different. And it's yet another way that cowards and misguided politicians are misinterpreting and misunderstanding what law enforcement training is all about. Most of the time, it has nothing to do with the actual training itself. The problems tend to arise because cowards want to appear "politically correct," or boldly revisionist, or whatever else they want to pretend to be for the moment.

Here's a specific case of how "politically correct" cowards get swept up in popular delusions and fail to provide the kinds of training that law enforcement professionals need the most—all because of labels and words. Lieutenant Colonel (retired) Dave Grossman has spent decades researching and lecturing about the kind of training that law enforcement professionals need to survive, and fight for their lives when necessary. Looking past his vast experience and tremendous accomplishments is like looking past a mountain. Yet some cowardly leaders believe—or more accurately, *misperceive*—that Grossman's training courses should be avoided because the course content is "inappropriate." And that's exactly what happened when Minneapolis Police Chief Medaria Arrandonda pulled officers from Grossman's "Bulletproof" training course.

In prohibiting officers from attending such training in the future, Chief Arrandonda explained:

> "After careful consideration, the Minneapolis Police Department has decided it will not be sending any officers to this week's Bulletproof training. While we hold the safety of our community members and our officers in the highest regard, our policing model is built on a community of trust. We do not want to attend any training that could, in any way, shake the foundation of trust."[33]

Never mind that some people in the "community" shoot and kill law enforcement officers. Remarks like this seem to suggest that we should be less concerned with officer survival and more concerned about "trust" apparently. And due to little more than a few "revisionist" complaints—from people with little understanding of the law enforcement profession—all of a sudden, Grossman's training has become controversial.

This situation became even more unbelievable, when the mayor of Minneapolis chimed in, and made law enforcement training somehow even more political. The mayor essentially demanded that officers be prohibited from taking part in Grossman's training whether on duty—or off duty without the department approval. And even more absurdly, the mayor also demanded that officers be prohibited from *any training* that had not been pre-approved—so much for watching YouTube videos, or discussing procedures with fellow officers in the hallway.

---

[33] Mara H. Gottfried, "Minneapolis Police Follow Ramsey County Sheriff in Pulling Officers from Controversial Training," *St. Paul Pioneer Press,* May 15, 2018.

This instance should underscore how things tend to go backwards whenever misguided politicians and cowardly police leaders get involved in training. And that's pretty much what happened in this particular instance. Unfortunately, however, Minneapolis isn't the only place where police training has devolved into an absurd war of words. It's happening in agencies all over America. Instead of asking and listening to the training that officers want and need, cowards and politicians are telling them not only what training they *must have*—they're telling officers what kinds of training they *must avoid*.

All of this—the bare minimum "minimum standards," the focus on what's politically popular instead of what's necessary, and the politically "correct" wars over words—does nothing but cause officers to resent training in general. This is the very last thing anybody needs, because all of us— everyone in every community—suffers whenever officers are improperly trained, and cowards are reluctant to do anything about it. Nonetheless, cowardly leaders and misguided politicians don't seem to understand the damage they are doing regarding law enforcement training. So it's up to Courageous Police Leaders to make that perfectly clear and do whatever is necessary to improve training standards and ensure that officers get the training—*the right training*—they need to handle one of the most important jobs in American society.

Defending Warriors & "Warrior" Training

When Minneapolis Mayor Jacob Frey banned Minneapolis Police Officers from taking "fear-based, warrior style" training both on and off duty, I shouldn't have been surprised.[34] Although I was perplexed by his description of "warrior training" as being "fear-based"—as if officers were somehow going to learn how to be more fearful and treat everyone as a threat.

In a sense, Frey's misunderstanding isn't entirely his own fault. As usual, cowardly police leaders have misled others, and have done nothing to set things straight. Cowards have let politicians and the media co-opt and confound the true meaning of the word *warrior*—which embodies everything we expect from law enforcement officers and courageous leaders.

Least of all, the term *warrior* encompasses acting with integrity, reasoning with empathy, disciplining with compassion, and demonstrating mastery in dealing with stress and stressful situations.[35] In various cultures throughout history, warriors were considered men and women with a character of courage, bravery, and the utmost integrity.[36]

---

[34] Danny Spewak, "Minneapolis Police Officers Now Banned from 'Warrior-style' Training," *NBC KARE11, KARE11.com*, April 18, 2019. See also, Andy Mannix, "Minneapolis to Ban 'Warrior' Training for Police, Mayor Jacob Frey Says," *Star Tribune*, April 18, 2019.

[35] Frank McLynn, *Heroes & Villains: Inside the Minds of the Greatest Warriors in History*, (Random House, 2009): 8.

[36] Pamela Toler, *Women Warriors: An Unexpected History* (Boston: Beacon Press, 2019).

Warriors defend the weak, and stand between good and evil. And the fact that a warrior has a duty to avoid violence—and defend themselves and others against violence when necessary—seems to have been lost on the politically ignorant.

So when I heard the lies about "warrior training," I was compelled to defend the honor of warriors, and training that is absolutely necessary in today's law enforcement environment. So I reached out to the leaders of the Police Officers Federation of Minneapolis. As the Director of Training at LawOfficer.com, I offered Law Officer's Online Training platform to them free of charge.[37]

It seems that Mayor Frey heard about the offer and felt compelled to respond. So he held a press conference and seemed even more adamant about his prohibitive training policy—and the discipline that would result in violating it. The mayor said quite a bit during the press conference. Although rather curiously, he made no mention of the term *warrior*. Perhaps he realized that "fear-based" training and "warrior training" are completely opposite. And even more astonishing, it seems he may have realized that an officer who fears everyone isn't a warrior—but a coward.

This may not be the greatest victory among the wars of words. But I'd like to think that Mayor Frey and others would agree that the last thing we need is more cowards wearing the badge—or becoming politicians.

—Travis Yates

---

[37] Andy Mannix, "Minneapolis Police Union, Mayor Frey Still at Odds Over 'Warrior' Training Ban," *Star Tribune*, April 26, 2019.

REALITY & REALISTIC TRAINING

Instead of all the nonsense and chaos, a more courageous approach to training should focus on reality—and all of the actual dangers and circumstances involved in law enforcement. That may seem like a no-brainer. However, it's absolutely shocking how cowardly leaders fail to accept the reality of the dangerous situations—and fail to provide realistic training. And it's almost unbelievable how politicians and legislators downplay the realities of law enforcement just to score political points and promote more "politically correct" training programs, while banning others.

Cowards can "reform," revise, and reprimand all they want, but that's not going to change the fact that law enforcement is a high-risk profession—a profession that is *inescapably contingent upon the erratic and irrational behavior of criminals.* And they can play with words, and (mis-)judge what's "appropriate" or not all day long. But that will never change how the one thing that makes the biggest difference in law enforcement is training—and plenty of it.

So what exactly does a more effective, more courageous approach to training involve? It starts by sticking with the facts, and training officers for the most challenging and most dangerous situations they may face, whether that involves deadly force encounters, safer driving tactics and habits, officer health and wellness, or other mission-critical aspects. And it should focus on a blend of theory and practice—and absolutely must involve the most realistic training possible.

The Reality of Gun-related Violence

For example, in facing reality, it's worth noting that more than 1,700 law enforcement professionals have died in the line of duty in the past 10 years. According to several sources, such as the Officer Down Memorial Page, about 30 percent of them were killed by gunfire. And according to the FBI, 55 law enforcement officers were killed in the line of duty in 2018—by 55 assailants.[38] Taking a closer look, 51 of these assailants used firearms to kill officers, and 4 assailants used vehicles as weapons to kill officers. And as far as percentages go, 93 percent of the officers who were feloniously killed in the line of duty in 2018 were killed by firearms; and the remaining 7 percent were killed by vehicles used as weapons.

Clearly, the leading cause of line-of-duty deaths in 2018 are the result of criminals shooting and killing law enforcement officers. This alone should settle any debate about why "warrior-like" training is necessary, and why firearms training, and training to deal with armed and dangerous subjects is absolutely necessary.

But that's only half the story. Aside from how these officers were tragically slain, there's another fact that shouldn't be ignored when it comes to training. Most of these assailants weren't first-time offenders—they had been arrested before, and some had extensive criminal backgrounds. It's a fact that cowards and social justice "warriors" and their allies seem all too eager to ignore.

---

[38] "FBI Releases 2018 Statistics on Law Enforcement Officers Killed in the Line of Duty," FBI National Press Office, May 6, 2019; see also https://ucr.fbi.gov/leoka/2018

Yet the fact remains that in 2018, 49 of the 55 assailants had prior criminal arrests—and 20 were under judicial supervision when they killed law enforcement officers. Yes, about 90 percent of the assailants had been arrested before and incidentally, 40 percent of the suspects had been previously arrested for weapons violations.[39]

So never mind the war of words about "warrior" and "bulletproof" metaphors. Refusing to accept the reality of these facts is a kind of negligence: it ignores criminal behavior and the significance of deterrence—and leaves officers without the training they need to overcome potentially deadly consequences.

Courageous Police Leaders need to resist, and take advantage of the enemies' ignorance. Linking up training programs—with the facts and circumstances about why such training is necessary—can be extremely helpful. Because no matter what cowardly leaders and politically-correct activists may believe, if gun-related violence is the leading cause of line-of-duty deaths among law enforcement professionals, then routine firearms training—based upon realistic conditions and circumstances—is absolutely necessary.

Realistic Training & Being Prepared for Gun Violence

Granted, most agencies require yearly "qualifications"—but *testing* should never be confused with *training*. The dynamics and circumstances of gunfights and gun-related violence must be studied and practiced regularly. And while practical firearms training should include things like rapid target

---

[39] United States Department of Justice, Federal Bureau of Investigation, "Law Enforcement Officers Feloniously Killed with Firearms; Judicial History of Known Offender Prior to Incident, 2009–2018," Table 46 (2018). https://ucr.fbi.gov/leoka/2018/tables/table-46.xls.

identification and acquisition, there's a lot to learn about theoretical aspects, especially considering how many gunfights are won or lost within a few seconds, and typically involve criminals shooting at law enforcement officers and killing them within 10 feet.[40]

For one thing, officers need better training in how to be prepared to "de-escalate" and just as prepared to fight—according to criminal behavior, compliance, and resistance of course. And having officers encounter (role-playing) subjects who comply, or resist, or fight, should be a part of any realistic training program in that regard. Such training may not sound like anything new, but with all of the political nonsense and "reforms" swirling around, it's going to take plenty of courage to defend the need for such training, get it funded, and actually see it through.

While training for the deadliest situations and deadly threats is paramount, of course, several other kinds of training are also necessary, and these should be prioritized as well. These include the following, just to name a few: driver training & traffic-related safety; crisis intervention training; officer health & wellness training; and medical aid training.

But no matter the subject, the approach also matters when it comes to training. And Courageous Police Leaders would be wise to provide as much reality-based, realistic training as possible—as often as possible. Strangely, realistic training, or more specifically, Reality Based Training (RBT), is one of

---

[40] United States Department of Justice, Federal Bureau of Investigation, (2018). "Law Enforcement Officers Feloniously Killed with Firearms; Type of Firearm and Size of Ammunition by Distance Between Victim Officer and Offender, 2018," Table 32 (2018). https://ucr.fbi.gov/leoka/2018/tables/table-32.xls

the most beneficial kinds of law enforcement training, it remains one of the most ignored. However, training in real-life situations in real-life environments is truly the only way to know how someone will act or react. And it's one of the few ways to gain insight and truly understand the kinds of decisions they will make on duty, in stressful conditions, and dealing with frustrating circumstances. It's also one of the few ways to monitor, track, and help improve practical skills and effective decision-making.

Ultimately, thanks to problems old and new, Courageous Police Leaders must take a more strategic and savvy approach to law enforcement training. And whether it's to make training a priority, or to prevent social justice "warriors" from denying *true warriors* the training they desperately need, we must approach training with a lot more courage. Overall, Courageous Police Leaders will do well by facing reality and the facts, linking them to the need for training, and demonstrating the consequences if such training is denied. And it's always advantageous to focus on realistic training programs that can help officers develop better training habits, while giving them skills and decision-making proficiency they can more immediately put into use.

Of course, like so many other aspects of law enforcement, this is easier said than done. Indeed, it's going to take courage, and plenty of sacrifice to improve law enforcement training overall and truly elevate the law enforcement profession. However, making a difference in providing more effective training doesn't always require a huge budget, or some grand initiative—especially since the worst training is no training at all.

PUSH BACK AGAINST "POLICY-MAKING"

Policy.

The word alone makes just about everyone in law enforcement cringe. Which says a lot about the ways policies are typically misused in law enforcement agencies throughout the country. When they're done right, *policies can be helpful and provide necessary guidance.* Although effective policies are becoming more and more rare. That's because instead of focusing on crime-fighting, many policies are being used by cowards as a means of punishment, and a way to placate social justice "warriors," police "reformers," and politicians for all the wrong reasons.

Having reviewed hundreds and hundreds of policies from agencies big and small across America, there seems to be three big problems with law enforcement policies and directives:

1. they are misguided, and written so that cowardly leaders can appear righteous or virtuous;

2. they aren't routinely reviewed and revised as necessary;

3. and when they're revised, it's often because of a knee-jerk reaction to a particular incident and focus on "correcting the past"–not preparing officers for the future.

Instead of focusing on crime-fighting, cowards use policies as a means of punishment.

THE PROBLEM WITH "POLICY-MAKING"

One of the biggest problems with law enforcement policies throughout America is that they're misguided. But it's not just the policies that are the problem — the problem is how they come about. Indeed, there's a big difference between developing effective policies the right way, and what we call "policy making" — the wrong way.

As many of us know, developing effective policies takes time and effort. It involves careful deliberation, seeking advice from experts, and getting feedback from the community. "Policy-making," however, has a lot more to do with misguided politics, ego-stroking, and self-servitude — all of which hurt, rather than help law enforcement and crime-fighting efforts.

How can you spot policy-making? Whenever a policy makes cowardly leaders and narrow-minded politicians look good — while making things even more complicated for law enforcement — that's a pretty good indication of policy-making. And when a policy reads as though cowardly leaders are set on making things ten times harder for officers — and a hundred times easier for criminals — that's a pretty clear sign of policy-making as well. All in all, policy-making is pretty much what happens whenever cowardly leaders, politicians, and police "reformers" try to appease demands for "justice" and (feigned) public outcry. And it's the written proof, if you will, of what happens when cowardly leaders focus too much on politics, and not enough on policing.

While some policies may seem bad, the consequences are usually even worse, and policy-making typically results in adversity for law enforcement officers in one way or another. For example, sometimes policy-making is just about flexing new-found power and authority, which often results in plenty of distraction and disruption when it comes to safety and fighting crime. For example, as the newly elected sheriff of Wake County (North Carolina), Gerald Baker issued a policy directive that bans deputies from wearing sunglasses while "conducting official Wake County business."[41]

Of course, we should always be suspicious of "there's a new sheriff in town" policies and the newly elected officials who make them. Giving Sheriff Baker the benefit of all doubt, his no-sunglasses policy *may be* well intended, if it was genuinely meant to encourage more direct eye-to-eye interaction, which some people may value. However, a no-sunglasses policy defies practically every other conceivable sense of logic, safety, and tactical advantage. And it seems foolish to even point out how such a policy overlooks how sunglasses help reduce glare so officers can focus and see better, or how sunglasses can help adjusting to shift-work between days and nights,[42] or that sunglasses can protect against UV radiation (as documented in medical journals since the 1960s). And never mind that while deputies are squinting with contorted looks on their faces, the people with whom they are speaking may be wearing sunglasses—so the whole face-to-face, eye-to-eye communication is

[41] "Wake County Sheriff Bans Officers from Wearing Sunglasses in Public," *Spectrum News North Carolina*, May 8, 2019.

[42] Mark R. Smith and Charmane I. Eastman, "Shift Work: Health, Performance and Safety Problems, Traditional Countermeasures, and Innovative Management Strategies to Reduce Circadian Misalignment," *Nature and Science of Sleep* 4 (2012): 111-132.

pointless. But whatever the intention, policies and directives like this do one thing exceedingly well: they provide excellent examples of misguided "policy-making."

Needless to say, instead of policy-making for the sake of whims, egos, and political favors, *or whatever other distraction*, Courageous Police Leaders should always focus on developing effective policies. That is, they should focus on developing and revising policies that aren't petty, distracting, or complicated, but helpful for law enforcement professionals and the communities they serve. And that's what effective police policies do; they focus on officer safety. They focus on protecting the public—and they focus on the most efficient and effective use of law enforcement resources.

But there's something else that effective policies typically do: they put criminals on notice. Of course, most criminals aren't getting together for brunch every Sunday to review the latest policy developments of their local law enforcement agencies. But don't be fooled. Criminals, especially repeat offenders, are often well aware of what law enforcement can and cannot do according to policy, either from the "word on the street" or first-hand dealings with law enforcement. And without a doubt, criminals exploit the kinder, gentler, feel-good policy "reforms" that result from policy-making to no end.

Here's a brief comparison that hopefully illustrates some of the key differences between "policy-making," and developing and maintaining policies the right way.

"POLICY-MAKING"	EFFECTIVE POLICY
Political, egotistical	Professional
Burdens and frustrates officers	Helps officers work more safely, effectively, and efficiently
Serves politicians, critics, activists, and "reformers"	Serves police officers & the community
Often a knee-jerk reaction to social and political pressure	Concentrates on the long-term scope of officer safety, protecting the public
Reducing crime and altering/deterring criminal behavior are an afterthought	Fighting crime and public safety are always the primary focus
Usually a cover up for failed political goals or political leadership	Solely used to improve law enforcement and public safety
Looks nice on paper; but is nothing less than disastrous in practice	Helps officers excel at doing their jobs—and helps them avoid hazards, problems, and distractions.
Focuses on what officers must do for cowardly leaders	Focuses on supporting law enforcement officers (and not over-burdening them with bureaucracy)

Figure 8. Comparison of some of the characteristics of "policy-making" versus developing effective policy.

KNEE-JERK POLICY REVISIONS

It's bad enough when cowardly leaders get distracted and initiate absurd directives and policies. However, knee-jerk "policy making" is also dragging the law enforcement profession to new lows all across America. Granted, it may be difficult to ignore how "people with signs" and Twitter followers have magically become influential nowadays. And with all the chaos that social justice "warriors," police reformers, and cowardly leaders create, each and every complaint, criticism, or opinion now automatically qualifies as a demand for "action"—and a policy revision. And you can tell there's absolute chaos when even some of the most courageous and most respected law enforcement leaders get caught up in knee-jerk policy revisions—and officers suffer the near-deadly consequences.

For example, Eddie Johnson, the Superintendent for the Chicago Police Department, has one of the toughest law enforcement jobs in America. Yet he notably serves with a rare blend of courage and compassion, and a sense of understanding that many courageous leaders should strive to achieve. But after outcry after outcry from social activists, intense scrutiny from the U.S. Department of Justice, and a whirlwind of political forces in Chicago, even Johnson was swayed to propose changes for the department's use of force policy—and not in a way that benefitted or helped protect officers.

More specifically, the proposed policy changes required members of the Chicago PD to use "de-escalation techniques to prevent or reduce the need for force when it is safe and feasible to do so based on the totality of the circumstances." The changes also limited the use of force, such as prohibiting an officer from using a Taser more than three times. Of course, we must ask, why not two or four times? And the answer may very well be that "three" is a magical, arbitrary number that most people seem to like because it *sounds* reasonable. But arbitrary numbers are the least of the worries when it comes to policy-making—especially when policies are out of sync with case law and decisions of the Supreme Court. Unfortunately, the Chicago Police Department learned this lesson the hard way, and only after a veteran police officer was nearly beaten to death by an "unarmed" man.

Shortly after the proposed policy changes were announced, Chicago PD officers had a violent encounter with a 28-year-old man named Parta Huff on October 5, 2016. Incidentally, Huff was in court that morning facing charges for pushing a police officer to the ground during a traffic stop. After leaving court, Huff crashed his car into a liquor store. And when Chicago PD officers arrived on scene, they spotted Huff walking away from the wreck. He seemed dazed and possibly injured, but as soon as officers approached, Huff became defiant and combative. Officers began to struggle with Huff, to no avail or advantage. Huff shrugged off getting repeatedly hit with a Taser, as though it were nothing. And as officers continued to struggle with Huff, he began to violently beat a veteran officer "like she was a punching bag," according to one witness.[43]

After a 10-1 "Officer Needs Assistance" call went out, plenty of officers arrived and ultimately subdued Huff. But not before he inflicted enough bodily harm and damage to send three officers to the hospital. The veteran officer suffered the worst: a severe concussion, wrist and neck injuries, and

---

[43] "Caught on Camera: Chicago Female Officer Savagely Beaten and Attacked by Suspect During Arrest," *CW39 Houston,* October 17, 2016.

bone chips to her shoulder. Huff, who was "unarmed" by news media standards, nonetheless repeatedly smashed the officer's head so hard that the concrete embedded in her face had to be surgically removed.

It was a nightmare of an incident. And all of the "de-escalation techniques" in the world were likely not going to stop Huff from nearly beating officers to death. The fact of that violent reality soon became quite clear. That night, Superintendent Johnson went to the hospital to visit the officer after her surgery. And that's when perhaps the most chilling part of this ordeal occurred. As Superintendent Johnson later explained to the media:

> "She looked at me and said… she thought she was gonna die. And she knew that she should shoot this guy. But she chose not to. Because she didn't want her family or the department to have to go through the scrutiny the next day, on national news."[44]

The officer was getting her face smashed into the pavement. She feared for her life. Yet somehow, she feared the scrutiny from the news media and the public even more. And if we look more closely at this unfortunate incident, there's something even more remarkable. It wasn't just the veteran police officer who chose not to shoot Huff—all of the other officers on scene chose not to shoot. And with the pending policy revisions and limitations on the use of force, it doesn't take much to speculate why the officers were perhaps hesitant to use deadly force—against deadly force—as a fellow officer was nearly beaten to death.

---

[44] Jeremy Gorner and Hal Dardick, "Citing Beating of Officer, Chicago's Top Cop Says Police Are Second-Guessing Themselves," *Chicago Tribune*, October 7, 2016.

This unfortunate incident also proves an important point about misguided policy-making: "de-escalation" works as a tactic—not as a policy. That's because despite whatever the news media and the public think, law enforcement does not control all the variables in any situation—or the behavior of irrational people with criminal and violent intent. And when law enforcement officers encounter violent criminal behavior—which is what law enforcement is supposed to do on behalf of the public—there isn't a "de-escalation" technique in the world that can stop someone like Huff who is enraged and dead set on smashing a police officer's face into the ground.

And here's where all the policy-making nonsense about "de-escalation" fails. In this case, verbal commands did not stop Huff. Physical restraint did not work. Pepper-spray did not work. Prolonged, repeated Taser deployments did not work. Repeated attempts by several officers to physically stop Huff from smashing an officer's face into the pavement didn't work. And yet, even though she was getting her face smashed into the pavement, the officer's worst fear seemed to be the bad publicity she might face for shooting Huff, so she was reluctant to use deadly force—to stop Huff's deadly force.

As Superintendent Johnson proclaimed with somber resolve, "This officer could have lost her life ... We have to change the narrative of law enforcement across this country"—and he's absolutely right. We must change the anti-police narratives. And Courageous Police Leaders must combat wayward "policy-making" at every turn, because far too many cowardly police leaders are responding to all the false narratives and chaos with misguided policy-making. Otherwise, as this example clearly proves, officers' lives will be put at even greater risk.

Yet this unfortunate incident also shows how Courageous Police Leaders can effectively combat policy-making nonsense. After the incident with Huff, Superintendent Johnson didn't waste any time doing his part to "change the narrative." Johnson boldly scrapped the proposed Chicago Police Department use of force policy.[45] And instead of "policy-making" based on political whims, consensus, and arbitrary conclusions, Johnson took up the "objectively reasonable" standard from case law as a basis for revisions.

Johnson did away with the confusing "de-escalation" mandate in the proposed policy, which would have required officers to somehow magically "prevent" the need for force — despite the actions and intentions of violent criminals, of course. Aside from sounding like something inspired by New Age philosophy, the proposed "de-escalation" requirement provides a great example of something that should never be written into policy:

> 4. <u>De-escalation.</u> Members will use de-escalation techniques to prevent or reduce the need for force when it is safe and feasible to do so based on the totality of the circumstances.

With ridiculous policy-making like this, even if officers survived a deadly-force encounter — without second-guessing themselves — they'd still have to reckon plenty of consequences. For example, this absurd policy specifies that officers "will use de-escalation techniques" — not just one *technique*, but *techniques*, as in more than one. Which means in court or a departmental investigation, or citizens' review — if you used just one, you're done.

---

[45] Dan Hinkel, "Chicago Police Ease Restrictions on Use of Force in New Draft Policy," *Chicago Tribune,* March 7, 2017.

And whenever "the totality of the circumstances" becomes the basis for judging whether it was "safe and feasible" for an officer to do so something, it's a recipe for disaster. Even worse, it leaves matters wide open to interpretation, and never-ending scrutiny and second-guessing—the very things that the landmark case of *Graham v. Connor* set out to avoid.[46] *Graham v. Connor* requires that an officer's actions "must be judged from the perspective of a reasonable officer on the scene, rather than with the 20/20 vision of hindsight." And it specifies that such judgments must consider "the fact that police officers are often forced to make split-second judgments—in circumstances that are tense, uncertain, and rapidly evolving—about the amount of force that is necessary in a particular situation."

Further, according to *Graham v. Connor*, the opinions of politicians, cowardly leaders, and "reformers" do not matter. Only "the perspective of a reasonable officer on the scene" matters for judging the use of force. Which explains in a nutshell why the enemies of law enforcement are doing all they can to support "policy-making"—it's a way to get around case law. And it's a way to gain the power to second-guess police officers fighting for their lives, and drum up allegations against them in lawsuits after the fact.

Using policy-making to get around case law can have dire consequences, as the Chicago PD example proves. And when policy-making causes law enforcement officers to second-guess themselves, they're more likely to hesitate and get themselves killed or injured—and that's why Courageous Police Leaders must take action and combat policy-making at every turn.

---

[46] William H. Rehnquist and Supreme Court of The United States. *U.S. Reports: Graham v. Connor et al., 490 U.S. 386.* 1988.

"POLICY-MAKING" IGNORES REALITY

Aside from using policy-making as a power grab, cowards often use it to blur reality. Even if you're not a big fan of political strategies and conspiracy theories, it's hard to ignore how policy-making seems a whole lot like brainwashing. To continue with our example, all the policy-making at the Chicago PD ignored the surge in violence in Chicago and elsewhere in America. In 2016, as the Chicago PD was about to limit the use of force, and mandate the use of "de-escalation techniques," 31 Chicago PD officers were shot at that year—an 82 percent increase in the number of shootings at officers from the year before. And 21 officers were killed in ambush attacks throughout America in 2016—the highest number of ambush attacks on law enforcement in nearly 20 years.[47] But once again, politicians, cowardly police leaders, "reformers," seemed to have ignored this reality.

Unfortunately, it took a real-life brutal beating of a veteran police officer to point out the absurdity of the proposed Chicago PD "de-escalation" policy. But ultimately, Superintendent Johnson did not let politicians and "reformers" dictate "policy-making." Like Superintendent Johnson, Courageous Police Leaders must stand up against "policy-making" and push back against policy mandates and "reforms" that compromise officer safety, and undermine safe, effective law enforcement. Indeed, policy-making is a form of chaos with dire consequences that no Courageous Police Leader should ignore. Besides, politicians and cowardly police leaders should never be allowed to sweep things under the rug, or get away with misguided

---

[47] Mark Berman and Kevin Uhrmacher, "Ambushes and Fatal Shootings Fuel Increase in Police Death Toll This Year," *The Washington Post,* December 29, 2016.

policy-making, especially when it may cause law enforcement officers to doubt themselves—and suffer the consequences.

That said, of course there's much wisdom in "picking your battles." And thanks to cowardly leadership, there are indeed plenty of policy-making battles to fight. However, as the Chicago PD example—and the reality behind it—suggest, it's perhaps best to focus on combating policy-making involving use of force and officer safety, foremost. At the least, it's a good place to start, and can do the most good in keeping officers safe.

DEFYING POLICY-MAKING "MANDATES"

Sometimes, politicians and "reformers" can frighten cowardly leaders into "taking action" and making a mess of policies and procedures on their own. Other times, politicians may try to mandate "policy-making" or heap pre-made policies on to law enforcement agencies under the guise of "best practices" or "common standards," or other such nonsense. Here too, Courageous Police Leaders must make a stand. And here's an example of how that can be done.

Perhaps you've never heard of Wellington (Ohio) Police Chief Tim Barfield. But you should, especially since his actions in fighting "policy-making" mandates serve as an example for Courageous Police Leaders everywhere. Chief Barfield took a stand against mandates that seemed more concerned with political posturing, than effective law enforcement. And let's just say that anytime a governor issues an executive order to create a task force, that results in another executive order, to establish an advisory board to "oversee the implementation of recommendations of the task force," you can be pretty sure that you're dealing with bureaucratic "policy-making." And you're certainly not anywhere near a situation where law enforcement agencies are free to enact policies that best suit the circumstances and crime problems in the communities they serve.

The intentions of such policy "task forces" may be good—but the results typically are not. In this example, Governor Kasich signed Executive Order 2014-06K to create the Ohio Task Force on Community-Police Relations— "after a series of incidents in Ohio and around the nation highlighted the challenges between the community and police."[48] Granted, it was more like *the community was challenging the police,* rather than the other way around. But cowardly police leaders are often too afraid to say so, and often try to avoid real conflicts whenever possible.

It's easy to see how "policy-making" often looks like a re-write about how police *should have* handled a particular incident in the past—without much consideration of the dangers, circumstances, and challenges law enforcement professionals may face in the future. And that's pretty much the basics of the Ohio Task Force and all the policy-making that ensued. Yet despite plenty of concerns, hundreds of law enforcement agencies throughout Ohio jumped on the "policy-making" bandwagon.

---

[48] See the Ohio Collaborative Community-Police Advisory Board, https://www.ocjs.ohio.gov/ohiocollaborative/; also "Ohio Task Force on Community-Policing," https://www.ocjs.ohio.gov/otfcpr/.

However, Chief Barfield wasn't having any of it. He spotted the "policy-making" nonsense from miles away. He explained how the Ohio policy mandates were "not based in fact" and were basically "a reaction to stuff that has been going on since Ferguson."[49] Chief Barfield also courageously summed up the politics and hypocrisy of "policy-making" quite well:

> "If you don't do what they want they'll try to shame and bully you into doing this... I haven't talked to a police chief in multiple counties who think this is a good idea."

Whether it was a good idea or not, more than 500 agencies in Ohio ultimately followed the mandates. Barfield, however, courageously did not. Of course, he could have easily followed along, but instead, he resisted. And he remained committed to the idea that the Wellington Police Department should develop policies that work best for them. Chief Barfield stayed focused on policing—not politics. And he pointed out the inefficiencies and ineffectiveness that policy-making often brings about.

In his own words, Barfield explained:

> "When I'm spending all my time complying with this stuff, I can't do all the other things I need to do... I don't owe them anything. I don't answer to the governor. I answer to the mayor and council, and have no legal reason to comply. We don't get one dime as far as compensation for our time complying with all of this."

---

[49] Jodi Weinberger, "Police Departments Look to Comply With New State Standards," *The Chronicle-Telegram*, January 18, 2017.

Perhaps somewhat hidden behind Chief Barfield's pushback are a few key points about effective policies. For example, law enforcement agencies should be wary of large, blanket-like policy mandates, which can become challenging, if not impossible to follow or put to good use.

If policies don't necessarily apply, or even contradict effective leadership and police work, then they shouldn't exist. Simply put, effective policies should always reflect what is best for law enforcement and the public. They should be used as guidelines—not excuses, appeasements, or means of discipline. If a policy or policy update has more to do with these kinds of things—and less to do with effective law enforcement and crime-fighting—then it's probably not a good thing, and probably shouldn't exist.

Similarly, when a policy gets substantial criticism from law enforcement personnel or the public, that should tell you something. Of course, everyone is not going to applaud or agree with everything all the time. And criticism and resistance are sometimes necessary, if not a welcome sign of progress. However, all too often cowardly leaders will ignore suggestions or criticism and just enact a policy, more or less for the sake of enacting or revising a policy—in other words, for all the wrong reasons.

That's why Courageous Police Leaders must push back on "policy-making" and policy mandates—and insist upon effective policies that make sense. And there are plenty of advantages to be gained in sticking with the facts, thinking ahead toward the future—and staying focused on policies that effectively serve the best interests of the community and law enforcement, but also keep criminals awake at night.

ROUTINE POLICY REVIEWS

Misguided policies are one thing. Outdated policies are another. And both can prevent law enforcement from effectively dealing with their current circumstances, whatever they happen to be. One thing to note is that "outdated" policies aren't ones that were just written awhile back. It's perfectly fine for a department to still use a policy written in the 90's, so long as it's routinely reviewed—and still providing useful guidelines that are in sync with current law enforcements efforts.

However, some policies, even ones enacted a few months ago, may no longer reflect changes in criminal behavior, community expectations, technology, or case law. Knee-jerk "policy making" which attempts to respond to past events instead of helping officers deal with the future, is partly to blame. And failing to routinely review policies is just asking for trouble, especially during times of "reform" frenzy. So to avoid all the chaos these problems can cause, Courageous Police Leaders must ensure that policies are routinely reviewed, even when it may not seem necessary.

Granted keeping up with case law, federal, state, and local laws and other aspects of policy can be daunting. But nothing can be worse than being caught off guard or "surprised" when something goes wrong, or when a lawsuit arises from policies that are outdated, or out of sync with the current realities of modern-day law enforcement.

KNOW YOUR LIMITS

If you can't fly—run. If you can't run—walk.
If you can't walk—crawl. But by all means keep moving"
—*Martin Luther King, Jr.*

Indeed, there are plenty of things to learn and know when it comes to the "art of war." You should know your enemy. You should know yourself. But there's another very important thing to know as well: your limits. Granted, *courage* and *limits* may not seem to go together—especially since when we think of *courage*, we often think of heroic men and women who save the day. Yet Courageous Police Leaders know that perhaps sometimes the most heroic thing you can do is save yourself. That doesn't mean throwing others under the bus. It means knowing your limitations at any given moment— and avoiding things that will put you at a disadvantage. It also means saving yourself from stupidity and refraining from soon-to-be-regretted decisions. And in trying to avoid mistakes and keeping yourself in check, the quote from Dr. Martin Luther King, Jr. is worth remembering. It says a lot about striving toward progress, and doing the best you can—within your limitations.

Generally speaking, this is how Courageous Police Leaders should operate. While striving for progress, you shouldn't sacrifice yourself and walk into the traps the enemies have set for you. And you shouldn't push ahead or push back so hard that you push yourself off the proverbial cliff. The law enforcement profession needs courageous leadership. And the loss of even just one Courageous Police Leader is a loss too great. Don't let it be you.

STAY ON THE RIGHT SIDE OF SUBVERSION

Knowing your limits will take courage and perhaps a different kind of personal strength. There will probably be many times when it seems impossible to ignore the cowards and the critics. But don't be fooled by their ignorance, or their attempts to trick you into playing their petty games. Only cowards win at cowardly games. And there is perhaps no sweeter victory for the cowards than to catch a Courageous Police Leader off guard.

There's plenty more to be said about avoiding traps in the first place. However, if you do get caught up, and we all do, how you handle yourself as a Courageous Police Leader after the fact can matter even more. Courageous Police Leaders don't react. They don't try to retaliate. Instead, they assess their limits. And they respond only if absolutely necessary, and only when it gives them more of an advantage—by putting the enemy at a disadvantage.

Courageous Police Leaders don't react—they respond. And they don't try to retaliate.

Be Courageous—Don't Take the Bait...

Believe me, I know from experience that in trying to do the right thing, we can end up doing the wrong thing, if we aren't careful.

In defending the law enforcement profession against yet another tiresome claim of discrimination and demographic disparity, I referenced juvenile crime and how the effects of growing up without a father, or a father figure, should seem alarming. My opinions weren't based on mere feelings about how things ought to be, they were informed by the perspectives of experts in sociology and criminal justice, along with various academic papers and plenty of statistics from government agencies.

For example, according to the U.S. Census Bureau, the number of children living only with their mothers, tripled from 1960 to 2016. And there's a hit parade of statistics from various sources that suggest 90 percent of runaway children are from fatherless homes; 85 percent of children with behavioral problems come from fatherless homes; and 80 percent of rapists with significant anger issues come from homes without fathers.

These aren't just anecdotes. These are correlations that should raise deep concern for law enforcement and our society overall. Of course, the statistics and the circumstances vary, and could be better or worse from one demographic category to another, one place or another, or even just one household to the next.

So I was floored when one particular media outlet took issue with my concern. They claimed that I was "inciting racial profiling" and discriminatory policing in speaking about fatherless homes.

To say that I was upset is an understatement. And to think that I would promote racial profiling—as a person, as a father, and a nationally recognized law enforcement professional—is an absurd accusation to say the least. Even though I knew better, and even though I should have calculated a response—or resisted giving any response at all—I reacted to the author in person when I saw him.

I put my reputation at risk with every word I spoke. And at the same time, I was giving a basically unknown media outlet and an even lesser-known reporter legitimacy, as though what they had to offer actually mattered. Indeed, I took the bait and fell into the cowardly ploy behind the sensational media spin. I knew better. And I should have realized that such efforts typically lack any sincere intent to truly make things better. And I should have recognized how they had everything to gain, and I had everything to lose in going below my standards of professionalism by responding to such nonsense.

I should have given the attention-seeking critics no attention at all. I should have upheld my own standards. And I should have easily spotted the provocation. And if you can learn anything else from my mistake, I should have not been so easily offended—by the absurdity or the hypocrisy. Indeed the enemies of law enforcement have plenty of tricks and tactics and they'll use all kinds of bait to trap you. I failed to realize how absurdity and hypocrisy were just bait. It certainly lured me in, and I let it offend my sense of rationality and professionalism, which is something that cowards, social justice "warriors," and other enemies of law enforcement are counting on to gain an advantage.

—Travis Yates

Unfortunately, there are plenty of examples of courageous, smart law enforcement professionals who overlooked the limits, who reacted and retaliated, and pushed themselves off the cliff, if not out of a job. For example, if you're in a police air support unit, don't fly obscene patterns to "retaliate" against your supervisors watching the radar screen.[50] While creative, this isn't the kind of artful "warfare" we need to wage against cowardly leaders. Such retaliation may make us feel better, for a moment. But whenever we typically overlook our limitations, we tend to also overlook the consequences, which in this case was unfortunate: two of the key members were removed from the air unit, a rare assignment that often takes years of hard work to achieve.

Of course, we could chalk this up to "don't do stupid stuff." But there's a bit more to it than that. Successful "warfare" involves being a bit more calculated, and being keenly aware of your limits. Courageous leaders also know what can be gained and won—and everything there is to lose.

To say that Courageous Police Leaders must be vigilant about knowing their limits, and aware of the advantages and disadvantages is quite an understatement. They should be hyper-vigilant, especially since many of the modern-day battles occur in the court of public opinion on social media, where the one with the most Twitter followers seems to "win" by default, or during shouting-match protests/counter-protests, where everyone except reasonable people seem to be in attendance.

---

[50] Tina Moore and Max Jaeger, "NYPD Pilots Flew $4M Plane in Penis-shaped Route to Troll Boss," *New York Post,* July 31, 2019.

It's never a good idea to "feed the trolls"—especially when you can ignore them and make them eat their own words instead. So be courageous and learn from the regretful mistakes that are out there. And in combating the cowards, the chaos, and the lies—much like practicing Sun Tzu's *Art of War*—always think carefully about when it's best to attack or gain an advantage, or when self-preservation is perhaps the most courageous move you can make.

So be courageous!—know your enemy, know yourself, and know your limitations...

AFTERWORD

There's a price to be paid for freedom and truth. Ironically, the United States of America has long been considered a beacon of freedom, yet cowards and cowardly police leaders seem to be doing everything they can so that you won't think clearly or critically. And it seems they'll do whatever it takes to prevent you from doing your job as safely and sensibly as you should.

Indeed, cowards don't want others to think for themselves. They don't want others looking at data and evidence. They don't want others to consider the facts. And they certainly don't want others revealing untruths and debunked myths. Cowards fear losing power, even more than they fear being wrong, or having to apologize, or having to do what is right. Indeed, the most dangerous threat to a coward is someone who has the courage to think independently and challenge their lies. That's why cowards rely heavily upon news and social media to spread lies and misinformation and create chaos. They need the smokescreens to hide the truth.

I'm humbled that you've read this far. But I want to be clear about a few truths that hardly appear in print. And if I may offer one last bit of encouragement, it's this: the law enforcement profession was never wrong.

When a violent criminal in Ferguson, Missouri committed a robbery and brutally attacked Officer Darren Wilson—and cowards and so-called social justice "warriors" began to lie about the facts—Wilson and the honorable profession of law enforcement were not wrong.

When Charlotte Police Officer Brentley Vinson courageously used deadly force to protect himself and others from a suspect who refused to drop a gun, Officer Vinson and the law enforcement profession were not wrong.[1] But the violent protests and accusations stemming from this incident, particularly those from the local chapter of the NAACP should underscore the truly desperate measures that social justice "warriors" and critics will use in trying to indict the law enforcement profession.[2] The head of the Charlotte NAACP chapter not only dismissed the suspect's violent history, but claimed that African-American police officers—like Officer Vinson—aren't black but "blue." Such a remark seems out of touch with the facts and actual circumstances of this case, yet says a lot about the intra-racial discrimination that African-American law enforcement officers have been unfairly subjected to for decades.[3] And it smacks of the class divisions within the African-American community that influenced "racial" unfairness in the criminal justice system,[4] but with a new twist: "black" criminals aren't the problem; "black" cops are the problem. Yet the fact remains that Officer Vinson was not wrong—and neither was the law enforcement profession.

---

[1] Michael Gordon, "District Attorney Exonerates Officer, Denounces Rumors in Killing of Keith Scott," *The Charlotte Observer,* November 30, 2016.

[2] John Bacon, "NAACP: Blacks 'Demonized' After Being Shot by Police. *USA Today,* September 28, 2016.

[3] Kenneth Bolton and Joe Feagin, *Black in Blue: African-American Police Officers and Racism* (New York: Routledge, 2004).

[4] James Forman, Jr., *Locking Up Our Own: Crime and Punishment in Black America* (New York: Farrar, Straus and Giroux, 2017).

And when Baton Rouge (Louisiana) officers responded to a convenience store where a 911 caller reported that Alton Sterling had threatened him with a gun, they weren't wrong–and neither was the law enforcement profession. Despite attempts to take Sterling into custody using verbal commands, control holds, and a Taser, Sterling did not comply. Instead, *he* continued to resist. And it wasn't until he continued reaching for his weapon that he was fatally shot. None of these facts mattered, that is until both the United States Justice Department and the Louisiana Attorney General declined to file criminal charges against the officers who were involved.

However, the problem with each of these cases goes far beyond right and wrong. And there's a lot more at stake whenever cowards and liars can mislead the public into believing that an officer shot someone with their hands up, or that an officer—who is more "blue" than "black"—murdered an innocent man. To combat the cowards, the chaos, and the lies, law enforcement professionals must join together and take a courageous stand.

The cowards and the social justice "warriors" may have won their share of battles in the past. But Courageous Police Leaders will win the war. And so long as there are cowardly leaders, and social justice "warriors"—and so long as there is a "war on cops"[5] and violent attacks on police officers— Courageous Police Leaders must combat the cowards, the chaos, and the lies. Because no matter what the self-righteous may say or want us to believe, the law enforcement profession is not wrong.

---

[5] Heather Mac Donald, *The War on Cops* (New York: Encounter Books, 2016); also Tomi Lahren, "Biloxi Police Killing Shows the "War on Cops" is Real," *Fox News,* May 8, 2019.

ACKNOWLEDGEMENTS

While my name may be on the cover of this book, putting it together would not have been possible if it wasn't for so many others.

I knew there was no walking away from saying what needed to be said in this book after I met Deputy Stacy Ettel. He was a victim of cowardly leadership—yet became an inspiration for Courageous Police Leadership. Nobody had the courage to stand up for Ettel in the five years after his incident and dealings with cowardly leaders. There is no way to undo the past and relieve the pain that he and his family endured. But I knew that we both needed to do something to protect the future of the law enforcement profession and help protect those who serve and protect others. Thank you Stacy, for your encouragement, boldness, and willingness to be a part of the Courageous Police Leadership movement. It would not have happened without you. And I am honored to know you, and work with you.

If Stacy was the inspiration for this book, I owe the finished product to my editor, JC Chaix. He graciously took on this project without any incentive to do so. A victim of cowardly police leadership himself and a great cop in a previous career, his work within these pages will hopefully leave indelible marks toward advancing the law enforcement profession for the benefit of our society. I am forever grateful for his honesty, mentorship, dedication, and passion to help others.

My family has been there for me with every step I have taken in my law enforcement career, and writing this book was no different. My wife, Traci, lost her father in the line of duty when she was just four years old.[140] I've learned so much from her dedication to the law enforcement profession through her loss, and the sacrifices she continues to make for our law-enforcement family. Traci has given up her career goals and put many of her dreams on hold for her family. She is a Courageous Leader that I owe everything to. I have survived and achieved because of her—and I am a better man for it.

My kids—Trevor, Tanner and Taygen—are the reason I get up every morning and aim to do better. I love them with every fiber in my soul. And while Courageous Police Leadership matters to me and the future of the law enforcement profession, it also matters for their future and the society they will inherit. The future stands before them and their generation. And I pray they get up every day and tackle it like warriors—with courage.

My parents blessed me with a wonderful childhood, and constant love and encouragement. My late mother was a consummate American patriot. She loved everything that law enforcement stood for. I miss her tremendously, yet I still feel her support each and every day.

---

140 "Second Lieutenant James Pat Grimes," Officer Down Memorial Page. https://www.odmp.org/officer/5772-second-lieutenant-james-pat-grimes.

And if I know anything about leadership, I learned it from my father. He was a college athlete, Vietnam veteran, and a courageous law enforcement leader—and I had the privilege to be his son. My prayer is that someday, I will come close to achieving something meaningful, the way my father meant so much to so many.

After my father, no man made a bigger difference in my life than Tulsa Police Officer Walt Milner. He had been a police officer for almost 30 years when I met him. He had plenty of seniority, but he chose to work at night with rookies like myself. As a 22-year-old cop, I was fortunate to be mentored by a legend. And Walt was a legend for his courage, yet also for enduring his tragic background. The things that Walt experienced as an African-American police officer in the 1960s would likely seem unimaginable to many people these days. Regrettably, Walt also suffered a devastating tragedy when his young daughter was murdered on a girl scout trip.[141] Although being around Walt, you would never know that his soul was permanently tortured by suffering and loss. I can't imagine the courage it took to get up every morning, put on a uniform, and deal with criminals like the one who killed his beloved daughter.

Walt Milner was one of the greatest leaders I have ever met—and he didn't have a single stripe on his sleeve, or bar on his collar. Yet he exemplified everything that a Courageous Police Leader should be. My dear friend and mentor died of a heart-attack in 1997, at the age of 53, just a few months after his much-deserved retirement. I miss Walt tremendously. I wish we could

---

[141] Tim Stanley, "The 1977 Camp Scott Girl Scout Murders," *Tulsa World,* April 16, 2019.

hang out and have dinner again, and talk about law enforcement, our families—and trucks. And I can only imagine what a truly courageous leader like him would say about the state of the law enforcement profession today.

In closing, there are so many people that have held out a hand to me and supported me through the years. Jason Simoneau, Keith Wenzel, Tony Miano, Kevin Navarro, Doug Larsen, Robert Haling, Dave Been, Michael "M.C." Williams, Jim McNeff, Jonathan Conneely, Duane Wolfe, Steve Gallemore, Chuck Humes, Roger Chasteen, Doug Wyllie, Mark Sherwood, Dale Stockton and "The Real" Brian Hill have invested so much in helping me and I am forever grateful.

No one does this thing called life alone, and I promise those that I have mentioned and those I have not, that I will spend the rest of my breaths on this earth doing for others what you did for me.

A FINAL WORD OF CAUTION TO
THE COWARDS & CHAOS-MONGERS

I hope this book makes it clear that cowards and enemies may take on many forms. From cowardly police chiefs, commissioners, and sheriffs, to the activists, the media, and social justice "warriors"—cowards and chaos-mongers can be found everywhere. And knowing first-hand how cowards operate, some of you have read this book, or maybe just a few pages and are ready to pounce. But this isn't just a book; it's an invitation for you to help the law enforcement profession.

I know some of you will misconstrue my intentions, my words, and my opinions. Some of you are so egotistical that you'll believe I'm talking about you—and mistakenly believe that you must respond and attack me personally. That's to be expected. And I also expect that I may be a target of your personal attacks because my opinions may "offend" you. And I fully understand that my intentions to help others will likely rile your hypocritical intent to cause harm. Nonetheless, I hope at some point may you realize that truly extraordinary things that can be achieved when you stop fighting with others—and start working with them.

In the meantime, you'll probably play all kinds of cowardly games—like take my words and opinions out of context, or make abstractions and accusations for whatever purpose you mistakenly believe is more important than trying to improve the law enforcement profession and the community. Your attempts are unnecessary and unfortunate—yet hardly unanticipated.

But keep in mind, what worked in the past, may not work well in the future. And if I may say this without sounding too proud, more and more Courageous Police Leaders are becoming better prepared to combat cowards, chaos and lies.

This book is for the courageous men and women in law enforcement who have been subjected to injustice, acts of violence, and public persecution—all for trying to make their communities better and safer.

So long as Courageous Police Leaders are out there, and the brave men and women of law enforcement are willing to serve a greater purpose than themselves, then I am willing to endure whatever personal attacks you can muster. So call me names, hurl the insults, shame me online, write negative book reviews. And don't forget to toss your plans to halt the future of my career onto the pile.

History proves that cowards ultimately lose. And by no means am I trying to boast. I am just a speck on the shoulders of those who have fought against cowardly behavior for centuries. But I'm just as committed to the idea that truth matters—and that unfounded accusations, lies and cowardly behavior should never be tolerated.

Ultimately, the choice is yours: you can clash and create nonsense and confusion; or you can cooperate with Courageous Police Leaders—and help truly make a difference.

Just don't say I didn't give you a choice—or that I didn't warn you...

ABOUT THE AUTHOR

Major Travis Yates began his law enforcement career in 1993. Since then, he has served the public in a patrol capacity for more than 20 years, along with other assignments in the gang unit, media relations, training, policy, education and special operations. Travis has been recognized internationally as a leader in law enforcement training, receiving the International Police Trainer of the Year Award by ILEETA. His training in risk management, officer safety and leadership has been given across the globe including 47 states.

He is the Editor In Chief and Director of Training with Law Officer, and founder of the Courageous Leadership Institute. He is one of the most prolific writers in law enforcement, having authored hundreds of articles for various publications including The Daily Caller and PoliceOne. Travis has also been interviewed about law enforcement issues by major media outlets, including CNN, USA Today, ABC News, Nightline and the Associated Press.

As a lifelong learner, Travis is committed to training and education. He holds a Master of Science Degree in Criminal Justice from Northeastern State University, and is a Doctoral Student with Liberty University. He is also a graduate of the 227th Session of the FBI National Academy.

DEDICATION

"God will not have his work made manifest by cowards."
—*Ralph Waldo Emerson*

This book is dedicated to my parents, who exemplified love, compassion, and resolve—which provided a foundation for courage to prevail...

"Major Travis Yates tells the cold, hard truth about combatting the destruction of our noble profession. This book is a must read for true leaders in policing."
—Lt. Bob Kroll, President, Police Officers Federation of Minneapolis

"This book provides a sense a relief that the "problem" in law enforcement today is not the profession but rather the incompetent and spineless administrators that occupy our offices."—Deputy Tyler First

"Major Yates is a proven police leader, writer, and exceptional trainer. He has skillfully put his experiences into this book for all ranks of police leadership."
—Sgt. Keith Wenzel, Dallas Police Department (Ret.)

"The title itself says so much because being a true leader requires true courage. Not simply physical courage, but moral, spiritual and personal courage as well."
—Lt. Randy Sutton (Ret.) Author, Speaker and Founder of The Wounded Blue

"The "Courageous Police Leader" is spot on. Travis understands how our profession is losing ground thanks to the environment that cowardly leadership creates."
—Sheriff Gareth Hoffman, Dickinson County, Kansas

"This book should be mandatory reading. It unapologetically exposes and offers solutions to the most serious problems in the law enforcement profession today."
—Sgt. Charles Humes (Ret.), 2018 Law Enforcement Officer Hall of Fame Inductee.

"Every person in law enforcement, from the Correctional Officer to the District Attorney, must read this book to better understand how we are on the front lines of a war between cowardice and courage that will define the future of our profession."
—Dr. Josh Turley, (Ret.) Commander, Tulsa County Sheriff's Department

"This book is not for the squeamish or fainthearted. I would compare it with a homicide detective watching an autopsy; necessary but not pleasant. But those looking for simple solutions will be pleased because the unrealistic demands on modern law enforcement are not complex moral dilemmas—but a simple need for moral courage."
—Charles "Sid" Heal, President, California Association of Tactical Officers; (Ret.) Commander, Los Angeles County Sheriff's Department

"Travis Yates hits the target with this book. Law enforcement is at a crossroads. And it is time to take a tough look at these issues, and time for all of us to respond."
—Captain Michael Howell

"The lack of genuine servant-leadership in our profession is nothing short both a cancer and contributor to the "War on Cops." Fortunately, Travis provides a must-read diagnoses, prescription and cure for what ails our profession."—Chaplain Michael "MC" Williams

"In a world of hypocrisy, lies and deceit, Major Travis Yates has emerged as the voice of truth. For me, as a former gang member, the truth that Travis reveals in this book is loud, clear and very much needed in our community today."—Tom Maynard, Forensic Specialist

"It's taken me almost 40 years in law enforcement to find someone that motivates and encourages others toward greatness in leadership the way Travis Yates does. The only leadership resource that may be better than his teaching, is this book."
—Sheriff Scott Walton, Rogers County, Oklahoma

"Travis Yates has the courage to identify and challenge terrible leadership traits. This book is a valuable guide for developing the servant leaders needed for the next generation of honorable and noble public servants."—Chief Tim Barfield, Wellington (Ohio) Police Department

"Police work is not a social experiment, yet too many cowards in the profession have turned it into a failed course in sociology. Fortunately, Travis offers valuable lessons about "policing how you want to be policed."—Lt. Jim McNeff (Ret.)

"Travis cuts to the core of leadership in a no-holds barred approach. If you want to know about leadership and grow in leadership, devour this book, take notes, and employ the principles. You will not be disappointed in the far reaching and life changing effects."
—Dr. Mark Sherwood, Functional Medical Institute; Sgt. (Ret.) Tulsa Police Department

"This book is exactly what every leader needs to read—and what cowardly "leaders" need to read—so they can realize what they're doing wrong."
—Sheriff Jesse J. Watts, Eureka County, Nevada

Made in the
USA
Columbia, SC